SIEM

UPDATED TRAVEL GUIDE

Adventure in Siem Reap: Exploring the Hidden Gems of the Gateway to Angkor Wat

TABLE OF CONTENTS

TABLE OF CONTENTS..3

INTRODUCTION..7

WELCOME TO SIEM REAP 10

Location and Geography..10

History...12

Culture and People...15

Weather and Climate (Best Time to Visit) 17

WHY YOU SHOULD VISIT SIEM REAP...................20

VISA AND ENTRY REQUIREMENTS 24

GETTING TO SIEM REAP 27

TRANSPORTATION OPTIONS IN SIEM REAP.......31

PACKING CHECKLIST AND ESSENTIALS............36

LOCAL CUSTOMS AND ETIQUETTE.....................39

HEALTH AND SAFETY ADVICE.............................49

COMMON SCAMS YOU SHOULD KNOW 52

USEFUL KHMER PHRASES AND WORDS 58

POPULAR ATTRACTIONS AND HIDEN GEMS 64

Angkor Wat – A Must-Visit Gem in Siem Reap 64

Cambodia Landmine Museum – An Underrated Gem in Siem Reap 65

Ta Prohm – A Serene and Enchanting Siem Reap Gem 66

Banteay Srey Butterfly Centre 67

Tonlé Sap Lake 67

Angkor Centre for the Conservation of Biodiversity . 68

Kulen Nature Trails 69

Preah Khan - An Enchanting Siem Reap Gem 70

Angkor National Museum 71

The Terrace of the Elephants 72

Srah Srang 73

Prek Toal Bird Sanctuary 74

Me Chrey 74

Bayon Temple 75

Angkor Silk Farm 76

Siem Reap Crocodile Farm 77

Angkor Thom 77

DAY TRIPS FROM SIEM REAP 79

A FOURTEEN-DAY ITINERARY FOR A VISIT TO
SIEM REAP 87

Day 1: Arrival in Siem Reap 87

Day 2: Angkor Wat Sunrise and Angkor Thom 87

Day 3: Ta Prohm and Angkor Temples 88

Day 4: Angkor Temples Continued 88

Day 5: Floating Village and Tonle Sap Lake 89

Day 6: Kulen Mountain (Phnom Kulen 89

Day 7: Angkor Temples and Sunset at Phnom Bakheng
.... 89

Day 8: Local Culture and Art 90

Day 9: Quad Biking and Countryside Tour 90

Day 10: Cooking Class 91

Day 11: Battambang Day Trip 91

Day 12: Bird Watching and Eco-Tourism 91

Day 13: Silk Farm and Shopping 92

Day 14: Departure 92

DINING AND CUISINE 93

Traditional Cuisine 93

Best Restaurants and Eateries 96

SHOPPING 105

Markets and Shopping Places 106

NIGHTLIFE IN SIEM REAP 113

Best Bars and Nightclubs 113

ACCOMMODATION OPTIONS 119

Best Neighborhoods to Stay 119

BEST TRAVEL RESOURCES 135

CONCLUSION 137

INTRODUCTION

Visiting Siem Reap was a dream I had harbored for years. As a seasoned traveler, I'd heard countless stories about the awe-inspiring temples of Angkor Wat, the vibrant culture of Cambodia, and the enchanting allure of this small town in Southeast Asia. Finally, my dream was realized, and my adventure in Siem Reap exceeded all expectations.

Arriving at Siem Reap International Airport, I was greeted by the warm smiles of the Cambodian immigration officers, a prelude to the genuine hospitality I would experience throughout my stay. The ride from the airport to my hotel served as a fleeting initiation into the delightful pandemonium of the city, as motorized rickshaws weaved through the lively streets, and the alluring scent of street delicacies gently permeated the atmosphere.

My first stop was, of course, Angkor Wat. As the sun rose over the horizon, I stood in awe of the temple's grandeur. The ancient stone structures, adorned with intricate carvings, seemed to come alive in the soft morning light. The reflection of the temple in the lotus-filled moat was a sight to behold, creating a magical and almost surreal atmosphere. I spent hours exploring the temple complex, climbing steep staircases, and wandering through corridors where history seemed to whisper in every stone.

Angkor Thom, with its imposing South Gate flanked by serenading musicians and lined with stone-carved giants, was another unforgettable sight. The Bayon Temple, with its enigmatic stone faces, left me with a sense of intrigue and wonder. Each temple had its own unique story to tell, and I was immersed in the rich history and spiritual significance that enveloped this sacred site.

Outside the temples, I discovered the charming town of Siem Reap. Pub Street, the epicenter of nightlife and street food, was a sensory explosion. The street was lined with bustling restaurants and bars, each one offering a different culinary delight. I savored a bowl of traditional Cambodian Amok curry, a symphony of flavors blending coconut milk, lemongrass, and spices, and sampled skewers of exotic meats and insects, all washed down with Angkor beer.

A visit to the Old Market, or Psar Chaa, was a journey through vibrant chaos. Stalls and shops selling everything from colorful scarves to intricate silver jewelry and local crafts abounded. The market was a treasure trove of souvenirs, and I couldn't resist picking up handmade textiles and beautifully crafted woodwork as mementos of my Siem Reap adventure.

One of the most memorable experiences of my trip was exploring the Tonle Sap Lake. I embarked on a boat ride through the stilted villages that were home to Cambodian families who lived off the lake's resources. Witnessing their daily life, including fishing and tending to floating gardens, was a humbling experience that shed light on the resilience and resourcefulness of the local people.

During my stay, I also made sure to attend a traditional Apsara dance performance. The graceful dancers, dressed in elaborate costumes, told stories from Cambodian mythology through their movements. It was a mesmerizing performance that added to the cultural richness of my visit.

Siem Reap is a destination that touches the heart and soul. It's a place where ancient history, vibrant culture, and warm hospitality come together to create an unforgettable travel experience. As I left Siem Reap, I knew that a part of me would forever remain in this enchanting town, and I was grateful for the memories and experiences that would stay with me for a lifetime. Siem Reap had not only met but far exceeded my dreams and expectations, leaving me with a profound appreciation for the beauty of Cambodia and its people.

WELCOME TO SIEM REAP

Location and Geography

Northwestern Cambodian city Siem Reap is a well-liked travel destination mostly because it's close to the stunning Angkor Archaeological Park, which is home to the well-known Angkor Wat temple complex. The topography and position of the city are essential to its history and allure.

Location:

314 kilometers (195 miles) northwest of Phnom Penh, the capital of Cambodia, lies Siem Reap, which is located in the Siem Reap Province. The city is well situated on the northern edge of Southeast Asia's biggest freshwater lake, Tonle Sap Lake. The border with Thailand is to the north of Siem Reap, and the city's proximity to this international boundary has greatly influenced its growth and history.

Geography:

Tonle Sap Lake: One of the region's most distinctive geographical features, Siem Reap is located close to the lake's northernmost point. Because it gives the locals access to fish, irrigation, and transportation, this lake is an essential part of Cambodia's environment. The lake grows considerably during the rainy season, transforming into a large body of water. It becomes smaller as the dry season approaches, releasing rich area for farming.

River Siem Reap: The Siem Reap divides the city in half as it flows through it. The river enhances the city's natural beauty in addition to providing water for it. With their stunning vistas, the riverbanks are home to a large number of hotels, restaurants, and commercial establishments.

Lowland Topography: Part of the wider Cambodian plain, Siem Reap is situated in a lowland region. Since the ground is somewhat level, it may be used for agriculture, particularly the production of rice, a key crop in Cambodia. The region's economy has long benefited from this lush terrain.

The verdant surroundings are typified by rice fields, palm palms, and an abundance of luxuriant greenery. The juxtaposition between the rustic, agricultural setting and the ancient temples of Angkor is one of the region's most distinctive and alluring features. The rural villages dot the area around Siem Reap.

Water Management: An essential feature of Siem Reap's topography is water management, given the city's close proximity to Tonle Sap Lake. The Angkor temples were constructed by the ancient Khmer civilization, which was also renowned for its highly developed water management techniques, which included a vast system of canals and reservoirs. The water levels around the city and the Angkor temples are now managed in part by contemporary infrastructure.

History

Prior to Angkor

There is evidence that the region around Siem Reap was inhabited as early as 1000 BC, and that the people who lived there were not too unlike from the local peasants in contemporary Cambodia.

The Period of Angkoria

With an estimated million inhabitants, the city of Angkor prospered and rose to become one of the biggest cities in the world between the ninth and thirteenth centuries. A chronology of Cambodian history

Despite being just 25 kilometers distant, Siem Reap was still a little town when Henri Mahout visited Angkor in 1860, which helped to popularize this ancient landmark in the West.

French Colony

Following a deal that the French and Siam made in the late 1800s, Cambodia fell under French protectorate status. The French started restoring the temples in 1907 and boosted tourism at the Angkor ancient site, which had just 200 visitors in the first three months of its inauguration. Along with this, Siem Reap was formally settled, and the French started constructing in the little town. Things to know about Cambodia's past

Since Siem Reap was the only location to stay while seeing the temples, the number of tourists visiting the Angkor temples increased along with the number of visitors to Siem Reap. The Grand Hotel d'Angkor debuted in 1929 and is still operational today, although under the Raffles name.

One of Asia's main attractions in the 1950s and 60s was the Angkor temple complex, and Siem Reap began to grow as the city's entrance. The civil war virtually put an end to temple tourism in the late 1960s, and Siem Reap's gradual rise also came to an end.

The Khmer Rouge

After Pol Pot's Khmer Rouge dictatorship gained power in 1975 and pushed the people of Siem Reap and all of Cambodia into the countryside, tourism came to a complete stop. During this

13 | S I E M   R E A P :   U P D A T E D
T R A V E L   G U I D E

time, the Grand Hotel D'Angkor, several of the colonial mansions, and the shophouses in the old market escaped the destruction of most of the town.

The city was restored by the Vietnamese, but many locals did not return until after Pol Pot's death in 1998. With the restoration of stability, Siem Reap's tourist sector started to flourish once again.

A Contemporary City Arises

Economic growth brought Cambodia back into the traveler's radar. Almost all of the tourists that come to Cambodia stay in Siem Reap, which is one of the towns that are expanding the quickest. Of these tourists, half go to the Angkor temples. It has grown from a little hamlet to a bustling contemporary metropolis with pubs and restaurants as well as a new wave of opulent boutique hotels that are springing up everywhere in the area.

Beyond being just a layover on the way to the temples, Siem Reap boasts a vibrant artistic enclave where innovators and artists seamlessly blend the old and new, a collection of stylish lodgings, and a culinary landscape celebrated as "vibrant and diverse" in the esteemed pages of the New York Times.

After it was constructed in 2006, the airport now handles close to 3 million passengers annually. Even with its recent rapid expansion, the Old Quarter still retains a large number of structures in the colonial architecture, and it has managed to preserve much of its culture.

Travel & Leisure Magazine ranked Siem Reap as the fourth-best city in the world in 2014.

Culture and People

Siem Reap boasts a distinctive and diverse culture, a blend shaped by its rich historical legacy, spiritual practices, and contemporary development. Let's take a closer look at the culture and the people of this captivating city:

Diversity and Language:

The heart of Siem Reap is a tapestry of cultural diversity, with its population primarily composed of the Khmer ethnic group, the predominant ethnic community in Cambodia. The official language here is Khmer, the vernacular of daily life for the local populace. Although English is commonly spoken within the tourism sector, Khmer remains the language that resonates most deeply with the people.

Religious Traditions:

The spiritual fabric of Siem Reap is interwoven with Buddhism, the city's predominant religion. It's not hard to spot the influence of Buddhism in the numerous temples and monasteries scattered throughout the city. Monks, in their saffron robes, are a common sight, diligently carrying out their religious duties, adding to the spiritual ambiance of the city.

Traditional Khmer Culture:

Siem Reap is a custodian of a rich and time-honored Khmer cultural heritage. This legacy encompasses the arts, including traditional music, dance, and the exquisite Apsara dance, which masterfully portrays Khmer mythology. Apsara performances are often featured in cultural shows, providing a glimpse into this artistic tradition. The city's architectural heritage is another gem in the cultural mosaic, with ancient temples and structures adorned with intricate carvings and breathtaking design elements.

Community and Family:

In Khmer culture, family is not just a mere concept but a cherished value. The extended family often resides in close proximity, fostering strong bonds and mutual support. The elderly are revered, and traditions that uphold family values are deeply ingrained. Communal events and gatherings play a significant role, reinforcing the sense of community and togetherness in the local culture.

In this dynamic city, the confluence of history, spirituality, and modernity has given rise to a unique and welcoming culture, inviting travelers to immerse themselves in Siem Reap's traditions and the warmth of its people.

Weather and Climate (Best Time to Visit)

Similar to many cities in Southeast Asia, Siem Reap experiences a tropical climate characterized by distinct dry and wet seasons. Travelers predominantly flock to Siem Reap during the dry season, but it's worth noting that the climate is generally conducive for visits throughout the year.

Dry Season:

The dry season in Siem Reap spans from November to April. During this time, the city basks in sunny, warm, and humid weather, with temperatures ranging from 25 to 35 degrees Celsius. For an ideal visit to Angkor Wat, the period from early December to late January, considered the winter season, is highly recommended. During these months, the skies are clear, and the temperatures are comfortably moderate.

This is the prime time to witness breathtaking sunrises and sunsets. Moreover, not only are the days cooler, but the nights are also pleasantly mild. The hottest month is April, coinciding with the Khmer New Year celebrations, and temperatures can soar above 35 degrees. Rainfall during the hot and dry season is minimal.

Rainy or Wet Season:

The monsoon or rainy season in Siem Reap spans from May to the end of October, bringing with it heavy rain showers. At the onset of the rainy season, it remains quite hot, but most of the rain occurs in the late afternoon or early morning. This is also the time when rice planting commences.

June, July, and August bring cooler temperatures, with rain predominantly falling in the evenings and at night. September and October mark the wettest months of the year. Rainfall can happen at any time, but this should not deter you from visiting Siem Reap. During this period, the landscapes and scenery take on a picturesque and serene quality, making October particularly attractive for photographers.

Flooding:

When traveling to Siem Reap, there's no need to fear natural disasters. The city is well-prepared for tropical storms, and earthquakes are not a concern. However, one factor to be mindful of is potential flooding. The river running through the heart of Siem Reap can overflow in September or October due to heavy rainfall, coupled with water from Phnom Kulen flowing into Tonle Sap Lake. But don't let this deter you from experiencing Siem Reap during the wet season. Wading through the water, observing children playing and embracing the flood, offers a unique and delightful perspective on Siem Reap.

Average Temperature and Rainfall:

April and May are unquestionably the hottest months, with an average maximum temperature of 35°C. In contrast, November, December, and January are cooler but still warm during the day, with temperatures reaching up to 32 degrees.

The majority of the rain falls during September and October, with an average of 21 rainy days in these months, indicating frequent rainfall. December, January, and February are notably dry periods.

WHY YOU SHOULD VISIT SIEM REAP

Here are some fascinating facts about Siem Reap that might convince to pay a visit:

The name "Siem Reap" holds a historical significance, denoting the "Defeat of Siam." It originates from a crucial battle that unfolded in the 17th century, where the Khmer king, Satha, emerged victorious against the neighboring Thai kingdom of Ayutthaya. This triumph marked a pivotal moment in Cambodian history, as it led to the restoration of Cambodia's independence.

Siem Reap is renowned as the gateway to Angkor Wat, the largest religious monument globally, and the city closest to this magnificent site. Each year, millions of tourists are drawn to Siem Reap to explore the ancient temples and marvel at their intricate carvings and architectural grandeur.

The temples of Siem Reap primarily trace their origins to the Khmer Empire, one of the most formidable and prosperous empires in Southeast Asia between the 9th and 15th centuries. The kings of this empire, ruling from the capital city of Angkor and its surroundings, were prolific builders of temples and palaces, leaving behind a breathtaking architectural legacy.

The Tonle Sap Lake, located a short distance from Siem Reap, plays a vital role in the local ecosystem. It is the largest freshwater lake in Southeast Asia and supports a rich diversity of fish, birds, and other wildlife, making it an essential environmental resource for the region.

Siem Reap is characterized by a tropical climate, meaning it experiences hot and humid conditions throughout the year. The optimal time for a visit is during the dry season, which spans from November to March when temperatures are milder, and the skies are clear.

In recognition of its extraordinary cultural and historical significance, Siem Reap, particularly the Angkor area, was designated a UNESCO World Heritage Site in 1992. This UNESCO status has not only promoted tourism but also fostered conservation efforts, ensuring that Siem Reap remains a captivating destination for generations to come.

As for the people of Siem Reap, the city boasts a population that is 95% Khmer, contributing to its homogenous and welcoming atmosphere. Beyond the ancient stone temples, Siem Reap is a vibrant hub of contemporary Cambodian culture, featuring creative arts, bustling markets, delectable cuisine, and warm hospitality, all while maintaining its cozy and provincial charm despite a thriving tourism industry.

The city is also celebrated for its production of world-class Cambodian silk, crafted using traditional techniques dating back thousands of years. Visitors have the opportunity to witness the entire silk-making process, from nurturing silkworms to dyeing and weaving threads on traditional looms.

In addition to its historical and architectural wonders, Siem Reap is a hub for contemporary arts, with numerous galleries and workshops that support young artists and preserve Cambodia's artistic heritage. Notable attractions include the Phare Cambodian Circus, known for its fusion of music, dance, acrobatics, and storytelling, as well as the efforts of Cambodian Living Arts, which promotes young performers and artisans.

Siem Reap also serves as a base for exploring the majestic Mekong River, which winds through nearby provinces. Boat tours offer the opportunity to visit remote fishing villages, flooded forests, and island pagodas, providing a firsthand experience of river life and revealing a different facet of Cambodia.

Finally, Siem Reap preserves remnants of the French colonial era when Cambodia was part of French Indochina. Architectural vestiges from this period blend provincial Khmer styles with European influences. Several old colonial shop-houses have been transformed into charming cafe-restaurants, adding to the city's atmospheric charm.

VISA AND ENTRY REQUIREMENTS

If you're considering a trip to Cambodia, it's essential to be aware of the visa requirements for entry into the country. Here's a breakdown of what you'll need:

Passport Validity: Your passport must have a validity of at least six months beyond your intended date of entry into Cambodia.

Visa Application Form: Part of the entry requirements involves filling out a visa application form..

Passport Photo: Along with your application, you should submit one passport-sized photo (2x2 inches).

Visa Fee: A visa fee must be paid as part of the application process.

Visa Type: For regular travelers with a valid foreign passport, the appropriate visa is the tourist visa (Type-T). This visa allows for a single entry and permits a 30-day stay upon your arrival in Cambodia.

Visa Extension: Should you wish to extend your stay, you have the option to do so for an additional 30 days. This extension can be obtained at the Cambodia Immigration Office.

Visa Validity: The visa is valid for use or entry into Cambodia within three months from the date of issue.

Visa Sticker: It's important to note that this visa comes in the form of a sticker, which needs to be affixed to an available visa page in your passport. It should be signed and stamped. It is not an electronic visa.

Visa Page: Your passport should have at least two vacant visa pages to accommodate the visa sticker.

Application Methods: You have the choice of applying for a Cambodian visa in person at the Cambodian Embassy, typically found in locations like Washington, DC. Alternatively, you can opt for the convenience of the Cambodian eVisa system for online application.

eVisa Details: The online visa, known as the Cambodia eVisa, grants a 30-day stay for tourism purposes. If your home country is not exempt from the visa requirement, you will need to obtain this visa.

Ease of Online Application: The Cambodia eVisa is often the simplest way to secure your visa. The online application streamlines the process, eliminating the need to visit an embassy or consulate or apply upon arrival at the border.

As a side note, it's worth mentioning that Cambodian immigration authorities at airports have implemented a system for collecting fingerprints upon entry. This is done through an inkless, electronic process.

For the most current and accurate information regarding Cambodian visa requirements and procedures, it is advisable to visit the Cambodia website at https://www.cambodiagovisas.com/requirements

GETTING TO SIEM REAP

There are several ways to reach Siem Reap, each offering its own set of advantages and considerations. Let's delve into the available travel choices:

Flying into Siem Reap:

Flying into Siem Reap is a common choice for many travelers. Siem Reap International Airport is conveniently located about 7 km west of the town center and is actually busier than Cambodia's capital city, Phnom Penh. Since there are no direct flights connecting Siem Reap to the West, you'll typically transit through an Asian hub. The most popular direct flights to Siem Reap often depart from cities like Bangkok, Saigon (HCMC), Phnom Penh, Guangzhou, and Singapore.

The airport serves as a hub for Asian airlines, and carriers like Air Asia, China Southern Air, Vietnam Airlines, Cambodia Angkor Air, and Sky Angor Asia Airlines offer flights to Siem Reap. While the airport's facilities are relatively basic, with a few cafes, shops, ATMs, and a foreign currency exchange, the terminal itself is modern and well-maintained.

Flying into Siem Reap is generally the priciest option but also the quickest. If time is of the essence and budget constraints aren't a primary concern, flying offers the most convenient means of arrival.

Note the Following:

Obtaining a Cambodian visa on arrival at Siem Reap International Airport costs $20 USD, and this option is typically available to citizens of most countries, but it's advisable to confirm this before your trip.

Many accommodations in Siem Reap offer airport pick-up services, often available upon pre-booking. Depending on your hotel or guesthouse, this service may be complimentary or cost up to $25 USD.

Official taxis can be found near the terminal, with a typical cost of around $9 USD to reach the city center. If you opt for a motorbike taxi, expect to pay between $3 and $7 USD. Tuk-tuks are not allowed to wait at the airport, but your hotel can arrange for one to pick you up.

If you plan to purchase a local SIM card for use in Cambodia, the airport is a convenient place to acquire one. After collecting your luggage, you'll find several stands selling prepaid SIM cards. These usually cost $4 or more and include call and data credit, with the option to purchase top-ups.

Getting to Siem Reap by Bus:

Traveling by bus is a popular and budget-friendly way to reach Siem Reap, particularly from major hubs such as Phnom Penh and Bangkok. The bus journey from Phnom Penh to Siem Reap can cost as little as $10 (or $23 from Bangkok), and the buses are surprisingly modern and comfortable. Since this is a well-traveled route, there's a wide range of bus companies to choose from, with departures available throughout the day.

Getting to Siem Reap by Boat:

Another alternative for reaching Siem Reap is by boat or cruise ship. Boats departing from Phnom Penh offer daily trips to Siem Reap, with prices ranging from $25 to $35 USD for a journey lasting 4 to 6 hours. These boat routes typically cater more to local travelers than tourists, so comfort and safety facilities might not be on par with your expectations. Boats from Phnom Penh have been known to experience breakdowns.

However, taking this route provides a unique opportunity to immerse yourself in the local lifestyle and experience life on the water. For those seeking a more leisurely and luxurious voyage, multi-day cruises traveling up the Mekong River can be considered. These cruises offer a 4- to 5-star luxury experience.

It's important to bear in mind that boat services do not operate during the dry season, from December through April, due to low water levels preventing entry into Siem Reap. Even in June, during our cruise, we had to disembark and take a bus for the final stretch of our journey because the boats couldn't navigate the waterways.

TRANSPORTATION OPTIONS IN SIEM REAP

When you find yourself in Siem Reap, it's essential to know the most convenient means of getting around, especially since public transport is not readily available. Here's a guide on transportation options:

Firstly, it's important to note that the currency in Cambodia is the Riel and the US Dollar. Many transportation services primarily accept cash, and locals often prefer payment in USD. Ensure you have small denominations when you acquire USD, as $1, $5, and $10 bills are typically sufficient for your needs.

Tuk-Tuks: Tuk-tuks, also known as remorks, are the most affordable and popular way to navigate Siem Reap. For short, one-way trips within the town, you can expect to pay around $2 to $3 USD. For instance, if you're traveling from your hotel to Pub Street, the central hub for dining and entertainment, a tuk-tuk ride is a convenient choice.

Tuk-tuks consist of an open-air carriage attached to a motorcycle, providing seating for up to four passengers. You'll find tuk-tuks abundantly in the town, making it easy to secure a ride. Before setting off, communicate your destination with the driver and agree on the fare.

Taxis: Taxis are a more expensive option in Siem Reap, and they are not as readily available as tuk-tuks. Hailing a taxi from the street may not be as straightforward, as they are less common in this town. If you require a taxi, it's advisable to have your hotel arrange one for you.

Walking: Walking is a fantastic way to explore Siem Reap, especially when you're exploring within the city. Despite the seemingly chaotic appearance of the streets, it's generally a safe mode of transport. However, it's a good practice to keep your bags in front of your body, as bag snatching, though rare, is a precaution worth taking.

Crossing the streets in Siem Reap requires a degree of confidence and commitment, given the chaotic traffic and the weaving of bikes through the streets. If pedestrians move with determination in a specific direction, the local riders tend to navigate around them. Hesitation can be unpredictable.

Getting to Angkor Wat from Siem Reap:

Angkor Wat is the primary attraction drawing people to Siem Reap. It's an extensive Archaeological Park covering over 400 square kilometers and housing more than 45 ancient Khmer temples dating back to the 9th century.

To reach Angkor Wat from Siem Reap, consider these options:

Tuk-Tuk: Renting a tuk-tuk is a popular and cost-effective choice, typically costing around $20 USD for a full-day service. A tuk-tuk driver can take you to Angkor Wat and transport you between temples within the complex. Given the vast expanse of the park (over 400 square kilometers), walking between temples is impractical, and a vehicle is necessary.

Bicycles: For those on a budget, bicycles are available and can be a great way to explore the park. Local bikes can be rented for $1 to $2 USD per day, while mountain bikes are available for $8 to $10 USD per day.

However, it's important to note that Cambodia's climate is hot and humid, and after hours of exploration and temple visits, cycling to the next site may not be the most appealing option.

In conclusion, Siem Reap offers various transportation choices, with tuk-tuks being the favored mode of local travel. When visiting Angkor Wat, renting a tuk-tuk with a dedicated driver is a practical and cost-efficient option. Walking can be a convenient way to explore the town, but be cautious when crossing the streets, and biking within the Angkor Wat complex is feasible for those who prefer a more independent and budget-friendly adventure.

Here are some helpful tips for your visit to Angkor Wat:

1. Tuk-Tuk Drivers vs. Guides:

Hiring a tuk-tuk driver is different from having a guide accompany you around Angkor Wat. Tuk-tuk drivers typically drop you off at one side of a temple and pick you up on the other when you're done. If you prefer to explore independently, you can do so.

However, if you'd like a guided tour, there are plenty of guides available at each temple to provide insights and information.

2. Official Angkor Ticket Centre:

There is only one authorized place to purchase entrance tickets to Angkor Wat, and that is the Official Angkor Ticket Centre. It's crucial to buy your tickets from this official source and not from unauthorized individuals or vendors.

This is the sole legitimate ticket vendor.

3. Ticket Purchase and Timing:

Your tuk-tuk driver can take you to the ticket office on the day you plan to enter the park. However, if you intend to witness the sunrise, you must obtain your tickets the day before, typically after 4 pm.

Buying your ticket after 4 pm allows you to enter the park for free on that same day to catch the sunset.

4. Ticket Types and Duration:

Angkor Wat tickets are available in three options: one, three, or seven-day passes. It's advisable to opt for more than a one-day pass if you wish to explore the entire park, particularly if you intend to experience both sunrise and sunset.

For this reason, many visitors choose the three-day pass, which remains valid for any three days within the 10 days following your first visit.

5. Dress Code and Etiquette:

Dress respectfully when visiting Angkor Wat, as it is both an archaeological site and a temple. Ensure that your shoulders and knees are covered, as you may not be allowed to enter some of the temples if you're not dressed appropriately. Additionally, smoking is prohibited on the premises.

PACKING CHECKLIST AND ESSENTIALS

Here are some recommendations for what to pack for your trip to Cambodia, covering various aspects from luggage and clothing to handy gadgets and toiletries:

Luggage:

Consider a wheeled backpack, as you'll often use minibuses and coaches to travel around Cambodia. Luggage space is usually sufficient, so packing light is advantageous.

Bring an anti-theft day pack to safeguard your belongings, as pickpocketing can be an issue, particularly in urban areas.
Clothing:

What to Wear

Cambodia's dress code leans towards the conservative side, especially outside major cities like Phnom Penh and Siem Reap. When entering temples, ensure your shoulders and knees are covered at a minimum.

Emulate the locals by wearing long, loose-fitting clothes made from natural fibers. Jeans are commonly worn year-round, although the climate can make them uncomfortably hot.

There's no need to dress up, even in upscale restaurants and bars. Sandals and t-shirts are generally acceptable attire. Opt for long, lightweight pants, natural fiber t-shirts, and a light linen or cotton overshirt.

Ladies, bring plenty of cotton underwear, as larger sizes can be challenging to find in Cambodia.

Consider quick-dry clothing for loungewear or sleeping, although it may not be your first choice for everyday wear.

Have slip-on sandals or slides for the convenience of removing your shoes, and enclosed shoes if you plan on hiking or visiting local markets. A lightweight, breathable raincoat is a wise addition due to Cambodia's unpredictable rain.

Toiletries:

Carry biodegradable wet wipes, insect repellent with DEET, and store your toiletries in a transparent case for convenience.

Handy Gadgets:

Include a USB stick, memory card case, personal safety alarm, alarm door stopper, portable bicycle lock, delicates wash bag, sink stopper, Tide To Go Pen, and a dry bag for various needs during your trip.

These recommendations will help ensure you have a comfortable and prepared journey in Cambodia, covering everything from your attire to essential gadgets and toiletries.

LOCAL CUSTOMS AND ETIQUETTE

Understanding local traditions and etiquette is essential to having a meaningful experience in Siem Reap, even if visiting the city may be a cultural adventure. The distinctive fusion of Buddhism and Khmer culture in Cambodia greatly influences the social mores that visitors need to abide by.

While there are a few cultural practices in Cambodia that vary from those in the West, if you're a generally kind person, you shouldn't have any trouble blending in while you're there. Nonetheless, they are really prevalent, and even if you overlook one or two, travelers' gaffes are usually overlooked.

Salutations and Conversations

Learning the appropriate welcomes is the first step in navigating the landscape of Cambodian social etiquette. Imitating the locals might help establish a connection and demonstrate respect for their way of life. The "Sampeah," or traditional Cambodian welcome, is putting your hands together at chest height and bending slightly.

This motion may be used to indicate farewell, thank you, or even apologize in addition to greeting. Try studying the natives; they utilize varying degrees of Sampeah based on rank and age; the more respect is shown; the higher the hands are raised to the forehead.

Observe that while women still often choose "Sampeah," handshakes have grown more commonplace among males mostly as a result of Western influence. It's customary to reciprocate these courtesy offers in order to further your cultural immersion while you're there.

Respecting Senior Citizens

Respecting elders is highly regarded in Cambodian culture and is a crucial component of social relationships. It is traditional to give an elderly person a little bow or make the "sample" motion of folding your hands in prayer.

This gesture honors their expertise and experience while demonstrating respect. It's crucial to speak to elderly folks politely and to refrain from interrupting them. Being patient and paying close attention are often seen as respectful behaviors.

When engaging with seniors, there are some physical gestures that should be avoided in addition to showing verbal respect. It may be considered impolite to touch someone's head or give them a pat on the back, particularly if they are elderly.

It is also not recommended to cross your legs while sitting in front of an older since this might be seen as impolite.

Conversing with People of the Other Sex

It is crucial to respect cultural customs in Cambodia while engaging with people of the other sex. Particularly in public contexts, humility and respect are highly valued in Cambodian culture.

It's crucial for travelers to abstain from any actions that can be seen as impolite or improper. This indicates that until you have developed a deep personal connection, you should avoid making intimate gestures or physical contact with someone who is the other sex.

Men and women should also dress modestly and refrain from wearing anything too exposed, especially while visiting temples or other places of worship where modest clothing is customarily worn. You may make sure that your interactions with people in Siem Reap are courteous and culturally sensitive by keeping these practices in mind.

Dress Code & Suitable Clothes

It's crucial to dress appropriately while touring the temples and the city of Siem Reap.

Putting on Civil Attire in the City

It is crucial to dress appropriately while visiting Siem Reap. Since modesty and conservative dress are valued in Cambodia, it is advised to avoid wearing skimpy or exposing apparel when out and about the city.

Visitors who respect their culture and dress accordingly are well-liked by the locals. When exploring Siem Reap, it's essential to respect local traditions by covering your knees and shoulders.

You may completely immerse yourself in the rich cultural experience that this little city has to offer by choosing attire carefully.

Putting on Proper Attire in Temples

It's crucial to dress correctly while visiting Siem Reap temples as a demonstration of respect for the indigenous way of life. Since modesty is valued in Cambodian culture, it is advised to refrain from visiting temples in skimpy attire or bathing costumes.

Wear clothes that cover your legs and shoulders instead. It might be useful to have a scarf or sarong on hand in case you need to cover yourself while touring the temples. This not only shows reverence but also contributes to preserving the calm environment in these hallowed places.

Buddhist temples are very important in Cambodia, thus it's important to visit them with appropriate manners. As a gesture of respect, never forget to take off your shoes before entering temple structures.

Temple Manners and Conduct

The following conduct and manners should be kept in mind while visiting Buddhist temples in Siem Reap:

Cover your knees and shoulders to show modesty. It is deemed impolite to wear shorts, miniskirts, or sleeveless shirts.

Before you enter the temple grounds, take off your shoes. Traditionally, you would either leave them outdoors or bring them with you in a bag.

It is considered impolite to point your feet toward monks or Buddha statues. Sit cross-legged or on your knees as an alternative.

To preserve the tranquil mood inside the temple grounds, talk quietly and at a low volume.

Before taking any pictures, particularly of monks or worshipers, make sure you have their permission.

Unless specifically advised differently, do not touch any of the temple's hallowed items. Respect one another by avoiding close proximity and making no physical contact.

Be mindful of proper conduct at religious rituals. Take your cues from the locals and make sure you are doing correctly by seeing how they behave.

Steer clear of boisterous discussions or excessive sounds that can annoy those who are concentrating or praying.

Give goods or cash only if you really want to help maintain the temple. However, it is crucial to do so covertly and without looking for a reward.

Getting to Know Buddhist Monks

Knowing how to behave politely among Buddhist monks is crucial while traveling to Siem Reap. As monks are held in high regard in Cambodian culture, it is important to treat them with the appropriate deference.

Remember to show humility by lowering your head slightly when you approach a monk. Additionally, it's traditional to give or receive anything from a monk with your right hand. Furthermore, do not touch their hair or robes; physical contact is not appropriate.

You may make sure that your encounters with Buddhist monks in Siem Reap are courteous and suitable for the local culture by adhering to these etiquette recommendations.

Present-Giving Manners

Giving gifts is a significant part of Cambodian culture, thus visitors should be aware of the appropriate protocol. When presenting presents in Siem Reap, bear the following points in mind:

Recognize the Symbolism: Presents have symbolic importance in Cambodia. It's crucial to choose a gift that honors the recipient and demonstrates consideration. Traditional handicrafts, artwork, or little mementos are popular options.

Avoid giving extravagant presents; although it may be tempting, people often appreciate modest and thoughtful gifts more. Sincerity and care are more valued by Cambodians than a gift's monetary worth.

Give Presents With Both Hands: As a gesture of respect, it is traditional to use both hands while presenting a gift. This action demonstrates your humility and sincerity in giving the gift.

receive gifts with grace: It is appropriate to receive gifts from others with grace and to show your gratitude. It's crucial to express your thanks for the present, even if it falls short of your expectations or desires.

Steer clear of wrapping presents with white or black paper in Cambodian culture, since these colors are connected to death and sadness, respectively. It's advisable to steer clear of these hues while wrapping presents.

Think About Bringing Gifts For the Kids: Little toys or school materials are excellent presents that will be loved by kids and their families if you want to visit nearby towns or engage with kids while traveling.

Be Aware of Religious Convictions: Given the heavy Buddhist influence in Cambodia, cultural sensitivities should be taken into account while selecting a present. For instance, giving shoes as a present might be seen as impolite as Buddhists refrain from wearing shoes inside of temples.

Table Manners and Dining Manners

Be careful of Cambodian table manners and dining etiquette while eating in Siem Reap. Take note of these key reminders:

Wash Hands Before Consuming Food.

Hold off on eating until the host extends an invitation to have a seat.

To eat, use either your right hand or a utensil, generally a spoon. The act of using your left hand is generally discouraged.

With the exception of certain finger foods like spring rolls, avoid picking up food with your fingertips.

Try a little taste of everything that is provided by taking little quantities.

As a courtesy, the senior or oldest person at the table often begins eating first.

When chewing, keep your lips shut and try not to eat loudly.

It is considered courteous to consume all the food on your plate since it might be seen as wastage.

Say "soksabay" (pardon me) and indicate what you need if you need additional rice or another dish.

Chopping sticks should never be inserted vertically into a dish of rice because they will resemble the incense sticks used at funerals..

For visitors to Siem Reap, it is essential to comprehend and show respect for the traditions and manners of the locals.

Respecting Cambodian customs is shown by abiding by certain cultural standards, which range from greetings to proper attire in temples.

HEALTH AND SAFETY
ADVICE

Siem Reap is generally considered a safe city, even at night. However, if you decide to rent a bike, it's advisable not to keep your bag in the basket, as it could be an easy target for theft, especially by snatch-and-grab thieves. If you're a lone female and find yourself leaving late-night spots, it's a good idea to try to walk home with traveling companions, particularly if you're heading to poorly lit areas.

In Siem Reap, there are instances of commission scams involving certain guesthouses and small hotels that pay moto and taxi drivers to bring in guests. To avoid falling victim to this scam, consider booking your accommodations ahead of time via the internet and arranging for a pick-up. Another option is to stick with a reputable guesthouse if you're arriving from Phnom Penh. Alternatively, you can negotiate with the hotel or guesthouse upon your arrival.

Beggars are a common sight in Siem Reap, and some visitors may become fatigued by constant requests for assistance. It's important to remember that Cambodia lacks a robust social security network and government support, making life very challenging for the poorest of the poor. While you don't need to give to everyone you encounter, it's also essential to treat them with respect. When it comes to children, it's generally better not to encourage begging, but if you feel compelled to help, offering food is a more sustainable option, as giving money often ends up in the hands of someone else.

When visiting remote temple sites beyond Angkor, it's crucial to stick to clearly marked trails, as there are still land mines in certain areas like Phnom Kulen and Kbal Spean.

Cambodia is generally safer than some people might believe, but exercising caution is still necessary. Most incidents of violence occur among Cambodians, but there have been cases of muggings and even fatalities involving tourists in places like Phnom Penh and Sihanoukville. To protect your belongings and personal safety, it's wise to keep most of your cash, valuables, and your passport in a hotel safe. Additionally, avoid walking on side streets after dark. While Siem Reap has historically had lower crime rates than the capital, this is gradually changing. Late at night, it's best to avoid using motos, as moto theft is a prevalent crime in Cambodia, and the unfortunate drivers often face severe consequences.

Most major tourist destinations have had land mines removed from their vicinity. However, unexploded ordnance can still be a concern in less-visited temple areas. In these cases, it's highly advisable to only travel with a knowledgeable guide. As a general rule, it's not recommended to venture into uncharted territory in Cambodia unless you are certain it's safe.

Cambodia has a concerning road safety record, with accidents being common in the chaotic traffic of Phnom Penh and on the highways, where reckless driving is prevalent. The better the road, the riskier the driving. Seatbelts should be worn if available, and if you rent a moto, wearing a helmet is essential.

In conclusion, Siem Reap is a destination with a lot to offer, from the ancient temples of Angkor Wat to vibrant markets and cultural experiences. However, like any other tourist destination, it's important to remain vigilant against common crimes like pick-pocketing and bag snatching. Stay aware of your surroundings and take the necessary precautions to ensure a safe and enjoyable visit.

COMMON SCAMS YOU SHOULD KNOW

Tuk-Tuk Overcharging

Tuk-tuk drivers try to overcharge visitors, especially those who may not be aware with the local costs, is one of the most prevalent scams in Siem Reap. This is particularly common when visiting locations outside of cities where it might be difficult to locate local drivers. Before boarding the tuk-tuk, it is essential to haggle over the fee in order to prevent becoming a victim of this fraud.

As an alternative, you may think about utilizing a fixed-price ride-hailing service like Grab or PassApp. Also, watch out for drivers who could try to talk you into giving them more in tips. Although it's OK to tip for excellent service, it ought to be optional. For a smooth transaction, it is advised that you pay using the Grab app if you decide to hire a tuk-tuk through the app. It is crucial to remember that PassApp only takes payments in cash.

Fake Tickets

Selling counterfeit tickets is a typical fraud in Siem Reap. Travelers are the target of scammers who provide them with fake tickets or alluring offers that seem too good to refuse. Reputable travel companies or official ticket desks at the attractions are examples of approved marketers to avoid.

The safest and most dependable approach is to purchase tickets straight from the attraction's official website, if at all feasible. Getting authentic tickets from reliable providers can guarantee a smooth encounter devoid of any unpleasant surprises.

Fake Monks and Blessings

Fraudsters posing as monks are another prevalent fraud in Siem Reap. These impostor monks may come up to people and give blessings or ask for money to be donated to temples or good causes. It's crucial to remember that real monks don't aggressively solicit money or behave in this way.

It's advisable to give directly to reputable institutions if you want to support a temple or charity. Do some research and find reputable temples or nonprofit groups. This is to guarantee that the intended purpose of your donations is being met.

Unofficial Tour Guides

Then, another typical scam in Siem Reap involves illegal people posing as tour operators. These people could come up to you, particularly in the vicinity of the Angkor Wat complex, and offer their services at a reduced cost. Even while some people may know the bare minimum about the sites, they often need more training and in-depth information than certified tour guides can provide. Selecting an unlicensed tour guide might lead to an unpleasant and untrustworthy encounter, and you can lose out on important information and background information.

For a trustworthy and educational trip, always use authorized tour guides or respectable tour operators. After completing training, licensed tour guides can provide you with a greater knowledge of the cultural and historical value of the places you visit.

Fake Transport Services

Fake transportation services are a popular target for scammers in Siem Reap. In order to lure gullible tourists into making reservations with them, con artists may offer appealing rates for transportation services like day trips or airport transfers. These con artists could not provide the promised assistance, leaving you stranded or adding needless stress to your journey.

It is advised to make reservations for transportation services directly from your lodging or via reputable websites to avoid falling for this scam. In Siem Reap, a lot of respectable lodging establishments have their own transportation services or may suggest reliable ones. By making reservations via these reputable channels, you can guarantee a secure and dependable transportation experience.

Bicycle Rental Scams

Renting a bicycle is a fantastic opportunity to experience the independence of the open road and completely escape the tuk-tuk drivers. There may be a catch if someone claims you may park in front of their store, restaurant, or stall for free. Locals have been known to charge for parking, too. Make careful to lock up your bike and keep track of where you parked wherever you wind up parking, even if it ends up costing you several thousand Riel!

To ensure you don't get lost in the forest, it's also important to download maps offline, pin the temples you want to visit, and make sure your GPS is functional. Keep in mind that bags might be stolen, so avoid putting your bag in the bicycle basket.

Pushy Vendors

Anywhere there are visitors; there will usually be touts and pushy salesmen vying for your business, along with groups of kids shoving books, bracelets, and expensive water bottles into your hands. People will say or do anything to make a sale in this highly competitive environment, so it's wise to use caution when dealing with most information. Don't feel compelled to make any purchases at the entrance gate since there are food and drink sellers within the complex, despite what they may say.

Drive a hard bargain and be prepared to spend a little more for food and beverages than you would outside the complex. Before leaving town or within the temples, maps and guidebooks may be purchased for as little as US $1. However, try to avoid purchasing anything from youngsters at all costs, regardless of how adorable they may seem, since this supports a very dangerous practice.

Child Vendors

Many little children may approach you at Angkor Wat and attempt to tug at your heartstrings by begging you to purchase books or postcards or by claiming that they are in need of money for school. Avoid falling for it, even if they seem convincing. Sadly, youngsters are being pulled out of school and used as a source of revenue by their families or other people who take a significant portion, if not all of, of the earnings for themselves.

For good reason, there are signs all over the place warning against giving money to youngsters or beggars. They attempt to stuff other people's wallets and take advantage of visitors as much as they can, and every dollar they earn is just one more day they are not in school.

Being Secure

Try your best not to show off your possessions and store your camera before you start haggling. If you find yourself in the middle of a group of youngsters, keep a check on your pockets since it happens sometimes for wallets to vanish out of nowhere. Use common sense, avoid carrying large sums of cash or your passport, and be as watchful as you can with your possessions.

USEFUL KHMER PHRASES AND WORDS

Here are some useful Khmer phrases and words for visitors, categorized to help you during your trip to Cambodia:

Basic Greetings:

Hello - ស្ួស្ដី (sou s'dai)

Good morning - បុណ្យអូក (buenh au)

Good afternoon - បុណ្យល្ង (buenh lng)

Good evening - អាយន្ត (ai nte)

Good night - រាត្រី (raat)

How are you? - អ្នកសុខសប្បាយបំផុតឬ? (nek souk sabay bompoot ah?)

I'm fine, thank you - ខ្ញុំសុខសប្បាយបំផុត (khnhom souk sabay bompoot)

Polite Phrases:

Please - ស្ួម (som)

Thank you - អរគុណ (aw kuhn)

Excuse me - ស្ួមលើស (som lee)

Sorry - សំស្រលាក (som sralak)

Yes - បាទ (baat)

No - ទេ (tay)

Getting Around:

Where is...? - ...នៅណា? (...nai naa?)

How much is this? - ប៉ុន្មាន? (ponmaan?)

I want to go to... - ខ្ញុំចង់ទៅ... (khnhom chong taw...)

Taxi - តាក់ស៊ី (taksi)

Bus - រថយន្ត (rot tia)

Hotel - សណ្ឋាគារ (sathdtaan)

Restaurant - ភោជនីយដ្ឋាន (phetmaah)

Food and Dining:

Menu - ម៉ឺនុយ (menoo)

Water - ទឹក (tuk)

Rice - បាយ (bai)

Delicious - មានជាតិ (mean chey)

Bill, please - គណនេយ្យបូរី (koneiyu borii)

Shopping:

How much does this cost? - ប៉ុន្មាន? (ponmaan?)

I want to buy... - ខ្ញុំចង់ទិញ... (khnhom chong teun...)

Expensive - ថ្លៃ (gietlai)

Cheap - សប្បាយ (sabay)

Numbers:

One - មួយ (muoy)

Two - ពីរ (pii)

Three - បី (bei)

Four - បួន (boun)

Five - ប្រា (pra)

Ten - ដប់ (dop)

Emergency Phrases:

Help - ជំរាប (jomrap)

I need a doctor - ខ្ញុំចាំទូរទៅ (khnhom cham tur naa)

Fire - ភ្លើ (pley)

Police - ការបាល (kaa baal)

I'm lost - ខ្ញុំខ្លាស (khnhom khlas)

Common Expressions:

Yes, I understand - បាទ, ខ្ញុំយល់ (baat, khnhom yol)

No problem - គ្រប់គ្រង (krab krong)

What's your name? - ឈ្មោះអ្នកអត់? (chmeh neak at?)

Directions:

Left - ឆ្វាន (chhngnaa)

Right - ស្រឡាង (sralang)

Straight - ឆ្មាន (sralang)

Stop - ឈប់ (chhbab)

Turn - បក (baak)

Map - ផែនទី (pennthii)

Street - ផ្លូវ (plouv)

Time and Dates:

Today - ថ្ងៃនេះ (thngai ney)

Tomorrow - ថ្ងៃស្អែក (thngai saek)

Yesterday - ថ្ងៃមុន (thngai mawn)

Week - សប្ដ (saat)

Month - ខែ (khae)

Year - ឆ្នាំ (chna)

What time is it? - ម៉ោងណា? (mao ngaa?)

Emergencies:

I need help - ខ្ញុំត្រូវជំរាប (khnhom trov jomrap)

Call the police - ទូរស្សន៍ជាតិ (turtsaatsnei chaatei)

I've lost my passport - ខ្ញុំបានខុសឆាក (khnhom baan khos chhak chaak)

Health and Medical:

I'm not feeling well - ខ្ញុំមិនអស់ស្រួ (khnhom min asaa suor)

Where is the hospital? - ម៉ាត់បន្ទេកវិកាយណ៌នៅណា? (mahbchhaekvikaay ney naa?)

Pharmacy - ស្លាប់ថៃ (slab tay)

Allergies - ឆុន (chhoon)

Pain - ទំនឺប (tomnoeup)

Shopping and Bargaining:

Can you lower the price? - បងបញ្ចប់ខុសតិ? (bang bangchhaap khos tea?)

Too expensive - គិតថ្លៃខ្លើយ (gietlai khpuay)

Discount - បញ្ចប់ (bangchhaap)

I'd like a discount - ខ្ញុំចងបញ្ចប់ (khnhom chong bangchhaap)

Leisure and Entertainment:

Sightseeing - ការទស្សន៍ (kaatsatsnei)

Beach - ឆ្នាំង (chnaang)

Museum - សារមននាម (saamonaanama)

Show - បងស្រី (bang srei)

Nature and Environment:

Tree - ដើម (daeum)

River - ទប់ (tup)

Mountain - ភ្នែក (phnaek)

Lake - បឹង (bueng)

Sky - អាក (aa ka)

POPULAR ATTRACTIONS AND HIDEN GEMS

Angkor Wat – A Must-Visit Gem in Siem Reap

Why it's Amazing: It's highly unlikely that any traveler will make their way to Siem Reap and skip a visit to Angkor Wat, and for good reason! This UNESCO World Heritage site isn't just one of the most renowned attractions in Siem Reap; it's a global icon in Cambodia and Southeast Asia.

Constructed in the 12th century, it stands as the most extensive complex of Buddhist temples globally and ranks as the world's most significant religious monument, sprawling over 400 acres. Due to its vastness, you might find that one day is not enough to fully appreciate the magnificence of this place!

What to Do There: If you wish to explore the entire Angkor complex but aren't sure where to begin, hiring a tour guide is a wise choice. You can opt for guided tours that last for a day, three days, or even an entire week! Although a week could be fascinating, you might eventually experience "temple fatigue" by the end.

Cambodia Landmine Museum – An Underrated Gem in Siem Reap

Why it's Fantastic: This museum has a fascinating history. It was founded by a former Khmer Rouge soldier who collaborated with the UN to disarm and remove the landmines he had planted. What began as a personal collection eventually evolved into a museum as the interest from foreign visitors grew.

As the museum's curator expanded his collection by visiting local villages, he also started to care for orphans who had been impacted by the landmines. At present, several children are nurtured by the museum. It's one of the most enlightening sites in Siem Reap, offering insights into local life and history.

What to Do There: Delve into the history of the Khmer Rouge regime and its consequences on rural Cambodia, as well as how landmines are being addressed in the region. Remarkably, over 6 million landmines were planted in Cambodia. Depending on your timing, you may even witness some active landmine detonations.

Most importantly, you'll learn about the ongoing efforts to clear this part of the country, and you might even have the chance to meet some of the children who have benefitted from the museum and its programs. It's truly a must-visit attraction in Siem Reap!

Ta Prohm – A Serene and Enchanting Siem Reap Gem

Why it's Special: As part of the Angkor Wat complex, Ta Prohm might not make it onto your list if it were as well-maintained as the other temples in the area. However, it's its state of semi-neglect that makes it truly extraordinary.

If you've ever seen the movie "Lara Croft: Tomb Raider," you might think the temple scenes are mostly CGI, but no, it's a real place! Ta Prohm has been almost entirely engulfed by the surrounding jungle, giving it a haunting and captivating ambiance you won't want to miss.

What to Do There: Although it might seem like Ta Prohm has been left to decay, it has actually been preserved in a way that maintains its authenticity without compromising its structural integrity. While it may be tempting to channel your inner Indiana Jones, do exercise caution during your visit.

Additionally, be on the lookout for the enigmatic Ta Prohm dinosaur, a subject of ongoing debate over its authenticity!

Banteay Srey Butterfly Centre

Why it's Remarkable: If you have an interest in butterflies, this should top your Siem Reap itinerary, even surpassing Angkor Wat! This delightful butterfly sanctuary and conservation center houses thousands of butterflies native to the region, and the facility is designed to mimic their natural rainforest habitat, ensuring their comfort and natural behavior.

What to Do There: Get up close and personal with the enchanting Banteay Srey butterflies. If you're lucky (or unlucky, depending on your perspective), these colorful insects might land on you!

For those traveling with children, this is a must-visit spot. Beyond observing butterflies, you can partake in an interactive tour that educates you about the life cycle of these fascinating creatures. It's one of the most serene and tranquil points of interest in Siem Reap!

Tonlé Sap Lake

Why it's Fantastic: For a glimpse into traditional Cambodian village life, head to Tonlé Sap. Remarkably, more than 3 million people call the lake's shores home, yet it remains a serene and peaceful area in Cambodia. Various tours are available from Siem Reap, offering diverse activities. Kampong Khleang, the largest village on the lake, is located on the north shore and is renowned for its floating stilt houses and traditional handicrafts. The locals are incredibly welcoming!

What to Do There: Apart from the villages lining the lakeshore, Tonlé Sap boasts outstanding natural attractions. One of the highlights is the Prek Toal bird sanctuary, home to over 100 species of water birds.

Observation towers are available, but for a more immersive experience, you can row out onto the lake to get up close with the birds. Keep an eye out for other wildlife, including crocodiles, snakes, and turtles!

Angkor Centre for the Conservation of Biodiversity

Not only can you get up close and personal with Cambodian wildlife, but you can learn about breeding, conservation, and rehabilitation while you're at the center.

What to do there: You can visit the Angkor Centre for the Conservation of Biodiversity at any time, but the twice-daily tours at 9 am and 1 pm are highly recommended. Knowledgeable and friendly guides will walk you through the center's operations and the process of rehabilitating these beautiful animals. The journey to reintroduce sick and injured animals into the wild is long but highly successful at this center. Ensure you include this in your Siem Reap travel agenda!

Kulen Nature Trails

Why it's a Fantastic Choice: They say that the journey is just as important as the destination. When visiting Phnom Kulen Waterfall, it's truly about both! These picturesque hiking trails guide you alongside rushing rivers, past ancient temples, and eventually to a stunning waterfall.

While there are places to grab snacks near the waterfall, a delightful idea is to pack a picnic and savor it in this awe-inspiring setting. For hiking enthusiasts, this is one of the most evocative natural wonders in Siem Reap that you won't want to miss!

What to Do There: Kulen Nature Trails offer a rewarding day out, suitable for hikers of various levels. Consequently, it can get quite crowded, so an early start is recommended. This way, you'll encounter fewer visitors, and you'll hike during the coolest part of the day. If your trip coincides with the dry season, these trails should be high on your Siem Reap itinerary!

Preah Khan - An Enchanting Siem Reap Gem

Preah Khan, meaning "Royal Sword," is a captivating temple situated in the northeastern part of the Angkor Archaeological Park. Built by King Jayavarman VII, it holds a special place for tourists, being in close proximity to the Ta Prohm temple.

What makes it Special: Preah Khan is adorned with lush greenery, with an abundance of plants and trees surrounding the temple complex, enhancing its natural beauty. The primary deity worshipped here is Lord Buddha, particularly in the form of Avalokiteshwara. The temple is known for its vast size and features two grand entrances. Before it became a temple, Preah Khan served as the residence of the royal clan, adding a touch of majesty to the site.

Location: Preah Khan is located on the western side of the Jataka Baray, to the northeast of Angkor Thom, making it conveniently accessible from the Ta Prohm Temple.

Hours: Preah Khan is open to visitors from 5 AM to 6 PM daily.

Entrance Fee: You can enter the temple complex with an Angkor Archaeological Park pass, which is priced at USD 20 for a one-day pass, USD 40 for a three-day pass, or USD 60 for a seven-day pass.

Angkor National Museum

The Angkor National Museum provides a comprehensive overview of Angkor and Khmer civilization, offering visitors a chance to explore this rich history in one place. The museum showcases various displays depicting the diverse religious practices and royal aspects of the Khmer dynasty, along with inscriptions, carvings, and details about prominent Khmer rulers, showcasing the grandeur of this region during the pre-Angkorian era.

Location: Siem Reap

Hours: The museum is open from 8:30 AM to 6 PM during April to September and from 8:30 AM to 6:30 PM from October to March.

Entrance Fee: Admission to the Angkor National Museum costs USD 12 for adults and USD 6 for children below 1.2 meters in height. Guided audio tours are also available for USD 3 per person.

The Terrace of the Elephants

The Terrace of the Elephants is a remarkable archaeological site within the vast Angkor Thom ruins, offering a glimpse into historical marvels.

What's Fascinating About It: Part of the well-preserved Angkor Thom temple complex, the Terrace of Elephants once served as the platform from which King Jayavarman II observed his triumphant army's return. This 300-meter-long structure is adorned with intricate bas-reliefs featuring small figures and statues of elephants, dancers, lions, horses, soldiers, and more.

The terrace, measuring about 2.5 meters in height, features three primary platforms, with the north platform boasting the most stunning carvings. As you walk past life-sized elephant sculptures, you can't help but be awed by the craftsmanship of local artisans.

Location: Angkor Thom complex, Siem Reap

Hours: The Terrace of the Elephants is open from 5 AM to 6 PM.

Entrance Fee: To visit the Terrace of the Elephants, you need an Angkor Archaeological Park pass, which is priced at USD 20 for a one-day pass, USD 40 for a two-day pass, or USD 60 for a seven-day pass. If you have purchased a ticket for Angkor Thom, you do not need to pay an additional fee for the Terrace of Elephants.

Srah Srang

Srah Srang, constructed during the 12th century by King Jayavarman II, is a substantial lake covering an area of 700 by 300 meters. What sets it apart is its perpetually filled water and the lush greenery that envelops it. The courtyard of Srah Srang offers a panoramic view of the Angkor Archaeological Park, and the lake was built primarily with laterite and sandstone. At the entrance to the lake, you'll find a platform flanked by two lion sculptures, as well as a Garuda and serpent statues nearby. For the most enchanting experience, visit during sunrise or sunset.

Location: Angkor, Siem Reap

Hours: Srah Srang can be visited from sunrise to sunset.

Entrance Fee: As part of the Angkor Archaeological Park, Srah Srang is covered by the entrance fee, which is USD 20 for a one-day pass, USD 40 for a two-day pass, and USD 60 for a seven-day pass.

Prek Toal Bird Sanctuary

The Prek Toal Bird Sanctuary, spanning over 42,000 hectares, is nestled in the Battambang Province. A renowned eco-tourist destination, this sanctuary attracts rare species of water birds during the migratory season.

The sanctuary is situated within the Tonle Sap Biosphere Reserve, and it hosts various migratory birds, including Black-headed Ibis, Painted Storks, Milky Storks, Spot-billed pelicans, Fish Eagles, Greater Adjuncts, Lesser Adjuncts, and more.

Location: Battambang Province, Siem Reap

Best Time to Visit: The dry season from December to March is the ideal time to spot a plethora of birds at the Prek Toal Bird Sanctuary.

Entrance Fee: A fee of USD 25 per person is required for entry to the sanctuary, and boat tours are available for an additional cost.

Me Chrey

Me Chrey is a floating village on the banks of the Tonle Sap Lake, and a visit here provides a unique opportunity to experience the lifestyle of the local inhabitants. The locals mainly engage in rice cultivation and fishing, and a visit during the early hours allows you to witness live fishing activities. You can reach Me Chrey by boat or tuk-tuk from Siem Reap.

Location: The bank of Tonle Sap Lake, approximately 9 kilometers from Siem Reap.

Best Time to Visit: Me Chrey is accessible throughout the year, but sunrise visits are recommended for an ideal experience.

Entrance Fee: Boat rides to Me Chrey typically cost around USD 20 per person, while eco-tourism packages are available for approximately USD 70 per person.

Bayon Temple

Bayon Temple is part of the Angkor Archaeological Park and was constructed during the 12th century CE under the rule of King Jayavarman VII. It showcases a harmonious blend of Theravada Buddhist and Hindu architectural styles, with numerous towers adorned with striking stone faces carved on them.

The temple is dedicated to Lord Buddha, and it features a multitude of towers, each of which is intricately carved. You'll also find captivating bas-reliefs depicting various mythological stories.

Location: Located in the capital city of Angkor Thom, established by King Jayavarman, Siem Reap.

Hours: Bayon Temple is open from 5 AM to 6 PM.

Entrance Fee: Entry to Bayon Temple is covered by the Angkor Archaeological Park pass, which is priced at USD 20 for a one-day pass, USD 40 for a three-day pass, and USD 60 for a seven-day pass.

Angkor Silk Farm

The Angkor Silk Farm offers a fascinating opportunity to learn about the entire process of sericulture, from mulberry cultivation to cocoon formation, the application of natural dyes to silk worms, and the complete process of silk production. The farm also showcases the ancient weaving technique of Ikat weaving.

Location: Puok district, approximately 20 minutes away from Siem Reap Center.

Hours: The Angkor Silk Farm is open from 8 AM to 5 PM every day of the week.

Entrance Fee: Guided tours are available, and entrance to the farm is free of charge.

Siem Reap Crocodile Farm

The Siem Reap Crocodile Farm is home to nearly 300 crocodiles coexisting in a controlled environment. Visitors can observe these creatures and gain insights into their breeding and feeding routines through informative guides available upon request. A tour of the farm takes around 20 minutes.

Location: Siem Reap.

Hours: Tours are available from 9 AM to 5 PM.

Entrance Fee: The entrance fee for foreigners is USD 3 per person, while it's USD 0.25 per person for locals.

Angkor Thom

Angkor Thom stands as a remarkable historical and archaeological attraction, established during the 12th century by King Jayavarman II. It was the final and most renowned capital of the Khmer Kingdom. Built in the traditional Bayon architectural style, this site is constructed using abundant laterite and features massive naga-carrying figures on its five 23-meter-tall towers. The southern gate, showcasing representations of the "Churning of the Ocean" episode from Hindu mythology, is frequently used by tourists traveling from Angkor Wat to Angkor Thom.

Traditionally referred to as Prasat Angkor Thom, much of Angkor Thom has succumbed to decay over time, leaving behind colossal remnants.

Location: Siem Reap.

Hours: Angkor Thom is open from 5 AM to 6 PM.

Entrance Fee: As part of the Angkor Archaeological Park, Angkor Thom is covered by the entrance fee, which is USD 20 for a one-day pass, USD 40 for a two-day pass, and USD 70 for a seven-day pass.

DAY TRIPS FROM SIEM REAP

An Exciting Trip to Angkor Wat

The Angkor temples are unquestionably the primary attraction in Cambodia and are consistently ranked highly on the list of must-see sights.

On a day tour, you can see the following sites: Ta Prohm, a temple where nature has taken over to create an incredible ancient utopia; Angkor Thom, the last great capital of the Khmer Empire, which is home to 37 enormous smiling stone face towers; Angkor Wat, the most well-known Khmer temple, whose sheer scale rivals that of the pyramids; Terrace of the Elephants, where King Jayavarman VII once stood to see his triumphant army return; Terrace of the Leper King, home to the Leper King Statue.

Like every other day trip, you have to leave early in the morning, between 7 and 8 am. You may be picked up at the place of your choice by your local guide.

After that, you'll start your adventure. All of the locations listed above are included, along with a few others that you will pass by. You should return to your hotel about 4 p.m., depending on how quickly you pick up the pace and how long the trip takes. Nowadays, air-conditioned cars are a must for most trips, but if you want a more immersive experience, you may request a tuk-tuk. Children may participate in this activity to a great extent since you will be driving through the temples. Usually included is water. Lunch, however, is on your own. Thus, arrive ready.

Photo Excursion from Siem Reap

One of the best things to do in Siem Reap is this day excursion. The holy mountain range known as Phnom Kulen, often spelled Phnom Koulen, means "mountain of lychees." It is located 30 kilometers north of Angkor Wat and 48 kilometers north of Siem Reap. The Kulen Mountain is particularly sacred to Buddhists, Hindus, and the people of Cambodia in general. In 804 CE, King Jayavarma II established the ancient Khmer Empire here by announcing his country's independence from Java.

At nine in the morning, your local guide will pick you up from your accommodation in Siem Reap and take you up the mountain. The trip lasts for almost 1.5 hours, so it's really lengthy. So you may savor the fleeting glimpse of rural Cambodia at your leisure.

When you get there, you may explore the temple grounds and get a closer look at local life. After there, go to the 1000 Lingas River. The Phnom Kulen waterfall, which is 20 meters high, is the tour's main attraction. Here are some pointers for preserving breathtaking moments at the location. Don't forget to pack a swimming suit and towels in case you want to take a swim. Because there are so many picture opportunities, this trip is perfect for both couples and families.

Tour of the Kompong Khleang Floating Village

For those of you who want to see Cambodia up close and go off the beaten path, this day trip is a fairly non-touristy pleasure. If you decide to embark on this trip, you may view the locals going about their everyday lives, check out the market, have lunch with the locals, and visit Kompong Khleang, a floating hamlet.

You will check out of your Siem Reap hotel at 8:30 a.m. and go out into the stunning countryside, where you may bike through the villages on dirt roads. Along the route, you may also visit a seafood market.

You will arrive at the enthralling floating village of Kompong Khleang as you go. You will get to see a stilt home and be asked to have lunch with the villagers, which will be in Khmer. After that, you will be escorted to Kompong Khleang's Vietnamese floating hamlet, which is not like the rest of the area. Instead of being made of stilts, houses and other buildings, like the local store or school, are hung above the water by means of floating things. You should arrive at your hotel about 5 p.m. after an exciting day of touring.

Day Trip to Banteay Srei Temple

As was previously said, there is a ton of captivating temples in Cambodia, particularly in Siem Reap. Pre Rup, a Hindu temple honoring Shiva that was constructed as a state temple by King Rajendravarman; Banteay Srei, also known as Banteay Srey, a Hindu temple of red sandstone composition honoring Shiva and dubbed "the jewel of Khmer art"; and Preah Khan, a temple north of Angkor Thom constructed by King Jayavarman VII in memory of his father, are all expected to provide unforgettable experiences on this particular day trip.

You will leave your Siem Reap accommodation at 8 a.m. and arrive to Pre Rup, your first stop of the day, after that. Following your exploration of this magnificent structure made of sandstone, laterite, and brick, you will go to Banteay Srei. The most elegant architecture in Cambodia may be seen there.

You will go to Preah Khan after eating lunch at the temple on your own dime. There are some unexpectedly nice pieces, even if the World Monument Fund is now restoring them. And your day trip ends at Preah Khan. Still, there are a few probable deviations. Remember to wear sneakers and loose-fitting clothes with coverage for your knees and shoulders since you will be walking a lot.

Embark on an Excursion to Koh Ker and Beng Mealea in a Single Day

Koh Ker is an archeological site in rural northern Cambodia, 120 kilometers between Siem Reap and Angkor. From 928 to 944 AD, it served as the temporary capital of the Khmer Empire, which was ruled by King Jayavarman IV and King Harshavarman II. Of the two dozen monuments on Koh Ker that are open to visitors, Prasat Thom—a seven-tiered pyramid resembling an Aztec pyramid amidst encroaching vegetation—is perhaps the most famous.

Situated 70 kilometers northeast of Siem Reap, Beng Mealea served as the last resting place for the late King Suryavarman II. Because of his many victories, Suryavarman II was highly regarded as "the King of Victory." The Angkor Empire only collapsed at Dai Viet (modern-day Vietnam), but under his rule it grew to include the Pagan – Myanmar kingdom, the Malaysian peninsula, and the northern border of Laos.

A large portion of the information on his reign was lost after his death. Western explorers didn't really enter the jungle to discover the remains until 1965. With the formal establishment of a route leading to the location in 2003, the enigma surrounding Beng Mealea was revealed.

This trip begins with a pickup from your Siem Reap accommodation and travels to the ancient temple of Beng Mealea via the verdant countryside of Cambodia. You will enjoy a great picnic lunch after exploring the 11th-century remains surrounded by overgrown vegetation. After an hour's drive northeast of Siem Reap to Koh Ker, your tour will continue. You will spend your time there taking in the amazing temples, sculptures, and thirty enigmatic main constructions.

You will then be driven back to your hotel by a chauffeur. Due to the two locations' primarily woodland surroundings, this is not really appropriate for children. In Koh Ker, heed your guide's advice and exercise caution since certain places are not well defined.

Kayak and Oxcart: A Day Tour of the Countryside

With kayaks and oxcarts used in place of the typical tuk-tuks or boats, this day trip is somewhat unusual. This journey will take you into the heart of the green rice fields, where you may see pagodas, have a picnic by the lake, and sample some delicious but simple local snacks. At 8:30 in the morning, you go to a small rural market where you may sample some Cambodian delicacies.

You will soon be heading towards your destination once your tour guide picks you up at your Siem Reap hotel. You will get in a kayak and paddle onto the lake, a conservation area well-known for its fauna and birds, after your visit to the market. Take a rest on a neighboring island after approximately an hour and continue on your wildlife viewing.

After that, you'll get back in the kayak and go to a popular local picnic area so you can take in the views. We'll visit a nearby pagoda to round off the day before returning to your lodging at 4 o'clock.

Day Tour of Tonle Sap

Translating to "Great Lake," Tonle Sap is the largest freshwater lake in South East Asia, and it is linked to the Mekong River that runs throughout the whole country. Tonle Sap may expand to about double its initial 3000 square kilometer extent during the rainy season. It is regarded as one of the most prolific ecosystems and provides the majority of the food for Cambodia.

Your hotel will get your complimentary transportation for your excursion around 7:30 to 8:30 am. After a 30-minute trip, you will arrive at your starting point at Chong Khneas village, where you will board a boat and go through all of the floating communities as you pass by on the canals. You will visit a fish farm and crocodile cage after you have made your way through the mangrove and into the large lake. At eleven a.m., after your aquatic adventure, you will be returned to your hotel.

A FOURTEEN-DAY ITINERARY FOR A VISIT TO SIEM REAP

A 14-day itinerary allows you to explore not only the famous Angkor temples but also immerse yourself in the local culture and explore the beautiful countryside. Here's a detailed 14-day itinerary for your visit to Siem Reap:

Day 1: Arrival in Siem Reap

Arrive at Siem Reap International Airport.

Check into your hotel or accommodation.

Relax and acclimate to the local surroundings.

Day 2: Angkor Wat Sunrise and Angkor Thom

Wake up early and head to Angkor Wat for a breathtaking sunrise.

Explore Angkor Wat temple.

Visit Angkor Thom and explore the Bayon Temple, the Terrace of the Elephants, and the Terrace of the Leper King.

Enjoy an evening walk around Pub Street and the Old Market area for dinner.

Day 3: Ta Prohm and Angkor Temples

Explore Ta Prohm temple, famous for its tree root-covered ruins. Visit Banteay Kdei and Srah Srang.

Afternoon visit to Pre Rup or East Mebon temples.

Enjoy a traditional Apsara dance performance in the evening.

Day 4: Angkor Temples Continued

Head to Banteay Srei, known for its intricate red sandstone carvings.

Explore Banteay Samre temple.

Visit Preah Khan and Neak Pean temples.

Relax and unwind in the evening.

Day 5: Floating Village and Tonle Sap Lake

Take a boat trip to Chong Khneas, a floating village on Tonle Sap Lake.

Explore the local way of life and enjoy the scenic boat ride.

Return to Siem Reap and have a free evening to explore the city.

Day 6: Kulen Mountain (Phnom Kulen)

Embark on a Memorable Journey to Phnom Kulen National Park for a day.

Visit the River of a Thousand Lingas, the giant reclining Buddha, and Kulen Waterfall.

Explore the local villages and enjoy a picnic lunch.

Head back to Siem Reap as the afternoon wanes.

Day 7: Angkor Temples and Sunset at Phnom Bakheng

Visit lesser-known temples like Beng Mealea or Roluos Group.

Climb Phnom Bakheng for a panoramic view of Angkor Wat at sunset.

Day 8: Local Culture and Art

Visit Artisans Angkor to learn about traditional Khmer arts and crafts.

Explore the Angkor National Museum to gain a deeper understanding of the region's history and culture.

Enjoy a relaxing spa treatment in the afternoon.

Day 9: Quad Biking and Countryside Tour

Take a quad biking adventure through the Cambodian countryside.

Visit local villages, interact with villagers, and learn about their way of life.

Experience a homestay with a local family for a truly immersive cultural experience.

Day 10: Cooking Class

Participate in a Khmer cooking class to learn how to prepare traditional Cambodian dishes.

Enjoy the food you've prepared for lunch.

Afternoon at leisure to explore Siem Reap on your own.

Day 11: Battambang Day Trip

Take a day trip to Battambang, a charming provincial town known for its French colonial architecture and rural landscapes.

Visit the Bamboo Train, Phnom Sampeou, and the Killing Caves.

Return to Siem Reap in the evening.

Day 12: Bird Watching and Eco-Tourism

Explore the Prek Toal Bird Sanctuary and Tonle Sap Biosphere Reserve, home to diverse bird species.

Take a boat trip to observe the birdlife and learn about local conservation efforts.

Return to Siem Reap in the afternoon.

Day 13: Silk Farm and Shopping

Visit the Angkor Silk Farm to learn about the silk-making process.

Shop for souvenirs, including silk products, at local markets.
Spend your last evening in Siem Reap enjoying a fine dining experience.

Day 14: Departure

Subject to your flight's timetable, you could find a little extra time to indulge in some eleventh-hour retail therapy or explore more local attractions.

Check out from your hotel and head to Siem Reap International Airport for your departure.

This 14-day itinerary allows you to explore the magnificent Angkor temples, experience the local culture, and discover the natural beauty of Siem Reap and its surroundings. Be sure to adapt it to your interests and preferences, and always check the opening hours and availability of activities in advance.

DINING AND CUISINE

Traditional Cuisine

Here are 10 local cuisines in Siem Reap, Cambodia:

1. Bai Sach Chrouk (Pork with Broken Rice)

Bai Sach Chrouk is a popular breakfast dish in Siem Reap, consisting of grilled pork and broken rice. The pork is marinated overnight in a mixture of garlic, soy sauce, and fish sauce, then grilled over charcoal until crispy.

The broken rice is steamed and served with the pork, along with a side of pickled vegetables and a dipping sauce made from soy sauce, lime juice, and chili peppers.

2. Fish Amok

Fish Amok is Cambodia's national dish, and it is a must-try for any visitor to Siem Reap. It is made with a delicate steamed fish mousse flavored with Khmer curry paste, coconut milk, and herbs.

The fish mousse is steamed in a banana leaf cup and served with a side of rice and vegetables.

3. Lok Lak (Stir-Fried Beef)

Lok Lak is a popular stir-fried beef dish that is often served with a side of rice, fresh vegetables, and a dipping sauce made from lime juice, soy sauce, and chili peppers.

The beef is marinated in a mixture of fish sauce, soy sauce, garlic, and black pepper, then stir-fried with vegetables such as onions, carrots, and tomatoes.

4. Khmer Red Curry

Khmer Red Curry is a rich and flavorful curry made with a variety of spices, including lemongrass, kaffir lime leaves, galangal, and chili peppers.

The curry is typically made with chicken or beef, but it can also be made with vegetables or tofu. It is served with a side of rice and fresh vegetables.

5. Nom Banh Chok (Khmer Noodles)

Nom Banh Chok is a refreshing noodle dish made with fermented rice noodles, fish curry sauce, and a variety of herbs and vegetables.

The noodles are topped with a dollop of fish curry sauce, cucumber slices, bean sprouts, and mint leaves.

6. Prahok Ktiss (Pork Dipping Sauce)

Prahok Ktiss is a popular dipping sauce made from fermented fish paste, garlic, and chili peppers. It is often served with grilled meats, vegetables, and rice.

7. Samlor Machu Kroeung

Samlor Machu Kroeung is a hearty Khmer soup made with a variety of vegetables, including pumpkin, green papaya, green banana, long beans, eggplant, and bitter gourd leaves.

The soup is also flavored with Khmer curry paste, prahok, and pounded rice.

8. Samlor Machu Trey (Sweet And Sour Soup With Fish)

Samlor Machu Trey is a sweet and sour soup made with fish, tamarind, pineapple, and vegetables such as tomatoes, onions, and carrots. The soup is often served with a side of rice.

9. Lap Khmer (Lime-Marinated Khmer Beef Salad)

Lap Khmer is a refreshing salad made with marinated beef, lime juice, fish sauce, herbs, and chili peppers. The beef is typically stir-fried or grilled, then mixed with the other ingredients. Lap Khmer is often served with a side of rice or sticky rice.

10. Samlor Korko (Stirring Soup)

Samlor Korko is a spicy fish-based soup with lots of vegetables. It is made with Khmer curry paste, prahok, pounded rice, pork or fish, and vegetables such as pumpkin, green papaya, green banana, long beans, eggplant, and bitter gourd leaves.

Best Restaurants and Eateries

Siem Reap boasts a delightful array of restaurants and charming cafes to cater to every visitor's palate. You can explore a diverse culinary landscape, ranging from high-end Mediterranean cuisine to authentic Khmer dishes, even including some made from insects. Additionally, you'll find local delicacies such as Lok Lak stir-fried beef, Amok fish, and Khor pork. Moreover, Siem Reap offers a world of international flavors, including French, Mexican, Italian, Thai, and more.

Cambodia's local and traditional cuisine is a unique gem in Southeast Asia, making it a must-try while visiting the country.

Here's a closer look at some of the top restaurants in Siem Reap, Cambodia:

1. Malis Restaurant

Malis is an upscale dining establishment that proudly serves 'Live Cambodian Cuisine.' Located along Siem Reap Riverside, this restaurant offers a wide range of experiences, including a bar and lounge, private dining rooms, and an outdoor garden where Apsara dance performances take center stage.

The menu features Khmer specialties like fish amok, chicken or beef curry served in lotus leaves, Kapot, and Khor crab fried rice, alongside Cambodian rice and noodle dishes, desserts, fresh fruit, and beverages.

Address: Pokambor Avenue, Siem Reap Riverside, Siem Reap, Cambodia
Phone: (+85) 515 824 888
Opening Hours: 7:00 a.m – 23:00 p.m
Price Range: From $4.93 to $39.52 per dish.

2. Cuisine Wat Damnak

Cuisine Wat Damnak is an award-winning restaurant led by French chef Joannes Riviere. It stands out as one of the few places in Siem Reap where Khmer dishes are prepared with the precision and quality standards of French cuisine.

The restaurant, housed in a traditional Cambodian wooden house in Wat Damnak village, offers three distinct dining experiences: a stylish modern dining room downstairs, a traditional Cambodian-style upper floor, and a lush garden surrounded by tropical greenery. The restaurant's 5-course or 6-

course menu, priced between $24 and $28, changes every two weeks, showcasing a fusion of traditional ingredients and spices from Southeast Asia with European techniques.

Address: Between Psa Dey Hoy Market and Angkor High School, Wat Damnak Village, Sala Kamreuk Commune, Siem Reap, Cambodia
Phone: (+85) 577 347 762
Opening Hours: 18:30 p.m – 21:00 p.m
Price Range: From $24 to $44.

3. Embassy Restaurant

Embassy Restaurant is dedicated to providing customers with an exciting culinary experience and a fresh perspective on Cambodian cuisine. Their kitchen specializes in traditional Khmer dishes sourced from various regions of Cambodia, using seasonal ingredients.

Founded by the Kimsan twins, this establishment takes pride in empowering women in Cambodia, showcasing a passion for food and innovative experimentation with dishes. Embassy Restaurant also offers an extensive selection of beverages.

Address: Corner Street 5 Sangkat Mondul 1 Village, Siem Reap, Cambodia
Phone: (+85) 589 282 911

Opening Hours: 18:00 a.m – 23:00 p.m (Closed on Tuesdays)
Price Range: From $44 to $97.

4. Banlle Siem Reap

Banlle Siem Reap is a haven for vegetarians in Siem Reap. It captures the attention of vegetarian diners with its traditional Cambodian, Asian, and European vegetarian dishes. Housed in a traditional wooden village in Wat Bo, this local gem even cultivates its own organic vegetables and fruits for a healthy, eco-friendly dining experience.

Must-try dishes include quesadillas with guacamole butter sauce, vegetable amok with rice, and eggplant tempura. There's also a delightful selection of fruit and juice smoothies, ice creams, and sorbets featuring flavors like vanilla, chocolate, pistachio, coconut, passion fruit, and mango.

Address: Road 26, Wat Bo Village, Siem Reap, Cambodia.
Phone: (+85) 585 330 160
Opening Hours: 11:00 a.m – 14:00 p.m; 17:00 p.m – 22:00 p.m (Closed on Tuesdays)
Price Range: $1.5 - $5 per dish.

5. Damnak Lounge

Located within the Lotus Blanc Siem Reap resort, Damnak Lounge offers an exquisite selection of European and

Cambodian dishes, complemented by a well-curated wine list. The restaurant's stylish decor allows diners to choose between an air-conditioned room or dining on the breezy outdoor balcony.

 Highlights on the menu include grilled lamb with potatoes and rosemary sauce, cod filet with grilled eggplant, zucchini, and orange cream sauce, and a traditional Khmer-style vegetable curry. For those seeking a variety of local specialties in one meal, the Khmer Savory Taste Menu, priced from $18 to $25, is an excellent choice.

Address: 1st Floor of Lotus Blanc Resort, National Road 6, Kruos Village, Siem Reap, Kingdom of Cambodia
Phone: (+85) 15 483 222
Opening Hours: 18:00 p.m - 23:00 p.m
Price Range: $10 - $30.

6. Kroya by Chef Chanrith

Kroya Restaurant is a truly unique culinary destination inspired by the rich heritage of Shinta Mani. Here, your taste buds will embark on a journey through innovative flavors that blend international and local ingredients with an infusion of indigenous herbs and spices.

Among the culinary masterpieces you'll find at Kroya are deep-fried fish accompanied by a delightful medley of pickles and mango, as well as fermented pork paired with grilled eggplant and papaya salad. The menu boasts an array of options, but if you find it hard to choose, don't worry. You can opt for the 7-course Khmer menu, a tantalizing experience that lets you savor a diverse range of Cambodian cuisines in one sitting.

Address: Oum Khun Intersection and Road 14, attached to the Angkor Wing of Shinta Mani Angkor and Bensley Collection Pool Villas, Siem Reap, Cambodia.
Phone: (+85) 563 968 590
Opening Hours: 11:00 a.m – 22:30 p.m

7. Khmer Kitchen Restaurant

Khmer Kitchen Restaurant is a beloved family-run establishment with several branches throughout Siem Reap. It has earned a reputation for serving delicious and affordable Cambodian and Thai cuisine.

The menu features a selection of mouthwatering dishes, including beef amok, banana flower and pumpkin salad, and Korko soup. This local gem also offers a variety of beverages, including draft beers, imported wines, and cocktails.

Address: Corner of 2 Thnou Street and Street 9, Old Market, Siem Reap, Cambodia
Phone: (+85) 512 763 468
Opening Hours: 09:00 a.m – 23:00 p.m

Price Range: Starting from $2

8. Olive, Cuisine De Saison

Olive's Cuisine de Saison restaurant is a culinary delight that beautifully melds French, Mediterranean, and Khmer flavors, all served in an elegant setting. Housed within a meticulously restored colonial building next to Wat Preah Prom Rath, this fully furnished, air-conditioned restaurant boasts brick walls adorned with images of famous dishes and fresh flowers.

The menu at Olive, Cuisine de Saison changes seasonally, incorporating the best of French and Mediterranean cuisine with local seafood, chicken, and fresh greens. Noteworthy dishes include seafood pasta, goat's milk cheese salad, foie gras with boiled soybeans, and grilled European sea bass. For those seeking a budget-friendly option, the lunch set, which includes a starter, main course, and dessert, is priced under $20.

Address: Olive Street, Siem Reap, Cambodia
Phone: (+85) 561 678 994
Opening Hours: 11:00 a.m – 21:00 p.m
Price Range: $7.5 - $18.5

9. Abacus Restaurant

Abacus Fine Cuisine, established in 2004, is an elegant restaurant conceptualized by the acclaimed French-Khmer duo,

Ivan Tizianel and Lisa Ros. Featuring a modern fine dining room with all the conveniences and a tranquil tropical garden, Abacus Fine Cuisine also provides a private dining area for an intimate dining experience.

The restaurant offers an extensive array of international and local beverages, including wines, beers, a wide range of spirits, cocktails, fruit juices, and soft drinks.

Address: Abacus Lane, Krong Siem Reap, Cambodia
Phone: (+85) 512 644 286
Opening Hours: 10:30 a.m − 14:00; 18:00 − 23:00; Saturday, Sunday: 10:30 − 21:00.
Price Range: Starting from $8.5

10. Mahob Khmer Cuisine

The name 'Mahob' translates to 'ingredients' in Khmer, a fitting choice for this elegant Cambodian restaurant situated along the banks of the Siem Reap River. Housed in a converted traditional Khmer house that once belonged to a governor of the Peak Sneng district of Angkor Thom, the restaurant provides various seating options, including an air-conditioned dining room, a breezy patio, and a beautiful garden at the front.

A standout feature at Mahob Khmer Cuisine is the à la carte menu, where dishes are cooked on a 'hot stone' using ancient volcanic rock grilling techniques. The restaurant also offers engaging cooking classes for those eager to learn the art of preparing Khmer dishes.

Address: 137, Training Village, Group 3, Siem Reap, Cambodia.
Opening Hours: 11:30 a.m – 10:30 p.m
Phone: (+85) 570 926 562

SHOPPING

Shopping in Siem Reap is truly an enjoyable experience, offering a diverse range of opportunities. You can witness artisans creating their crafts in ateliers before you decide to make a purchase. For those interested in affordable couture fashion, there are options to get fitted for bespoke clothing.

Additionally, you can explore handcrafted gifts at the Made in Cambodia market, and yes, indulge in the occasional fun of haggling for quirky tourist souvenirs at the bustling markets.

To make the most of your shopping day, consider starting your morning at the Old Market. It's not just about the shopping; it's also a fantastic place for people-watching, immersing yourself in the local culture. Spend your day leisurely strolling through the charming boutiques and art galleries, where you might stumble upon unique treasures.

Finally, wrap up your shopping adventure by heading to the lively night markets, where you can continue your retail therapy and perhaps even pick up some last-minute finds.

Markets and Shopping Places

Angkor Night Market

The Angkor Night Market is a bustling hub of activity in Siem Reap, housing more than 240 vendors who offer a treasure trove of handcrafted Cambodian crafts. Established in 2007, this market comes to life after sunset and presents an extensive array of items, from exquisite handmade tapestries to intricate paintings, as well as carvings crafted from wood or stone.

What makes shopping here even more rewarding is that it supports the local community by keeping the proceeds within the region. Personal favorites, such as my cherished t-shirts, were discovered right at this market, just moments after I captured a photo. And, as is customary in many markets worldwide, you have the delightful opportunity to haggle with vendors over prices.

To put it in perspective, the cost of my two beloved t-shirts, which have certainly proven their durability, was a mere $2. The satisfaction I derive from wearing them: truly priceless.

Psar Chas (Old Market)

While Siem Reap's retail landscape is evolving with cute souvenir shops and high-end boutiques, the Old Market, or Psar Chas, at the heart of the town remains a vibrant center of traditional trade and commerce. This historic market boasts a diverse array of items for purchase, from silverware and silks to handicrafts, spices, stone carvings, and a myriad of other fascinating finds.

Navigating the labyrinthine aisles filled with these treasures is a journey well worth a few hours of your time. Approach the art of haggling with a calm demeanor and a polite smile, and you'll likely uncover some great bargains.

The Passage - Louise Loubatieres Gallery

Situated on the trendy Hap Guan Street, the Louise Loubatieres Gallery is a captivating concept store that can easily whisk you away for hours. This charming shop is located in Kandal Village, a compact neighborhood nestled between the French Quarter and the Old Market, which is fast becoming a burgeoning district for shopping, dining, and leisure.

Louise, the delightful owner, possesses a diverse heritage with Cambodian, French, British, and Vietnamese roots, which is beautifully reflected in her impeccable taste and passion for Southeast Asian arts, crafts, textiles, and design objects. Her store's curated selection features a captivating range of beautiful items.

What sets this store apart is Louise's openness to source pretty things from various places, not limiting herself to 'made in

Cambodia' products. Whether it's colorful lacquer bowls or exquisite textiles that double as table runners, you'll find a wealth of home wares here.

Trunkh

Trunkh is a distinctive concept store brimming with Cambodian authenticity. From vintage shop signs typically found in rural Cambodia to hand-crafted wooden oxen and buffalo carved by a farmer, you'll discover a cornucopia of Cambodian treasures.

 The shop's inventory ranges from kitschy tea towels adorned with iconic symbols and landmarks like Angkor Wat to whimsical fish-printed travel pillows and Christmas stockings shaped like elephant trunks.

All Cambodian-made products at Trunkh are either found, designed by the owners, or locally sourced. Situated on the increasingly trendy Hap Guan Street within the emerging shopping, dining, and entertainment precinct known as Kandal Village, Trunkh is a personal favorite spot in Siem Reap, and despite its compact size, you can easily spend hours here.

Wa Gallery

The quintessential Cambodian souvenir is undoubtedly the checked cotton krama that adorns the necks, heads, or waists of virtually every Cambodian you encounter. Kramas are famed for their versatility, serving a multitude of purposes—some ingenious, some endearing, and some simply functional. They are worn as fashionable scarves or symbols of national and cultural pride, draped loosely around the neck over a neatly pressed dress shirt.

Yet, venture into the villages, and you'll witness local farmers using kramas as sweat-wicking headbands, while village women employ them as headgear. Personally, I've even utilized mine as a belt. These trusty companions are handy for mopping away perspiration while exploring temples in the sweltering humidity. While kramas are readily available everywhere, the Old Market offers them starting at just $1.

However, these are typically made from a polyester-cotton blend and may not offer the same quality. For authentic, high-quality cotton kramas, Wa Gallery is an excellent choice.

Sombai

Located in the Wat Damnak area, Sombai Liqueur is the perfect destination for finding unique souvenirs or gifts. Sombai offers homemade liqueurs and artisan products within the charming backdrop of a Khmer house, alongside a well-curated souvenir shop. Here, you can sample 11 different liqueurs and 5 alcoholic jams before selecting your favorites to take home as keepsakes or gifts for loved ones.

Sombai Liqueur goes beyond the typical shopping experience by inviting you to join their cocktail class, where you can learn to craft your own drinks using their delicious liqueurs. It's an engaging and interactive way to spend a couple of hours while unleashing your creativity.

By the end, you'll depart with new skills and recipes to impress your friends. Don't miss this unique opportunity to savor and create remarkable cocktails.

Fair Trade Village

Situated across from Angkor Village Resort on Road 60, the Fair Trade Village offers a captivating array of authentic Cambodian arts and crafts. This handicraft center showcases handmade products from over 20 handicraft enterprises and hundreds of artisans from all corners of Cambodia.

Here, you won't find any mass-produced items; instead, it's the only permanent space dedicated solely to retailing genuine Cambodian-made handicrafts. Additionally, all the products are certified by the Angkor Handicraft Association, guaranteeing their authenticity. When you purchase authentic Cambodian handicrafts here, you're not just acquiring beautiful pieces; you're also contributing to the preservation of ancient skills and supporting the social and economic development of local artisans and their families.

Beyond shopping, the Fair Trade Center provides a firsthand view of age-old techniques and skills unique to local communities, with some items being handcrafted on-site. The warm and inviting ambiance fosters an environment where guests are encouraged to immerse themselves in the richness of Khmer artistic heritage. The Fair Trade Center offers additional services, such as overseas shipping and wholesale orders.

Made in Cambodia Market

The Made in Cambodia Market is a vibrant showcase of the most exceptional craftsmanship in Cambodia today. It draws the participation of internationally recognized artisans and designers, including Saomao, Rehash Trash, Friends International, and many more. Shoppers can indulge in high-quality artisan products and luxury goods while supporting a new generation of skilled craftspeople, fostering their skill development and providing direct income.

This market also offers live entertainment and artist workshops to create a dynamic and interactive atmosphere. The venue boasts an array of cafes, restaurants, and boutique shopping options, making it a one-stop destination for shopping and leisure.

Senteurs d'Angkor

Founded in 1999, Senteurs d'Angkor is a well-established brand in Cambodia, known for its products inspired by the rich scents and flavors of this beautiful country.

You'll discover a wide range of locally made products at Senteurs d'Angkor, including home fragrances, natural soaps, candles, spices, and teas. It's the ideal place to find a souvenir or gift for those who appreciate original and sustainable handicrafts that respect Cambodia's traditions, nature, and people.

NIGHTLIFE IN SIEM REAP

Best Bars and Nightclubs

As the sun dips below the horizon, casting its warm glow over the enchanting Angkor temples, the vibrant nightlife of Siem Reap city awakens. In the iconic Kingdom of Wonder, the options for a lively evening are as diverse as they are alluring, with a mix of pubs, clubs, and cocktail bars waiting to be explored.

Take a leisurely stroll down the bustling city streets, and you'll discover opportunities to enjoy a refreshing cold draft beer for just $0.75, dance the night away on the famous Pub Street, and even sample a fried tarantula if you're feeling adventurous. The Siem Reap nightlife scene caters to all types of travelers, promising an unforgettable night out in Southeast Asia.

Here are some top recommendations for bars in Siem Reap, where you can savor your Margarita or beer as the night unfolds:

The Angkor Wat Bar

Located on the lively Pub Street, this bar is a favorite among experienced Cambodia tourists. It's often the epicenter of the best party in town, with energetic music, reasonable prices, and a diverse and friendly crowd of revelers.

Address: Street 08, Sangkat Svay Dangkum Krong

Opening Hours: 1 p.m.

Funky Flashpacker

Part of a popular hostel, this bar is renowned for its backpacker crowd who keep the party going all night long. Staying at the hostel might not guarantee a peaceful night's sleep, but it does promise a fantastic time at the bar. With affordable yet quality food and drinks, along with exceptional service, you won't find a negative review of the staff and bartenders here.

Address: 319 Funky Lane | Steung Thmey Village, Svay Dangkum Commune, Siem Reap 17259

Opening Hours: All day!

Miss Wong Cocktail Bar

Frequently featured on Siem Reap's top bar lists, this bar offers a unique and moody ambiance inspired by late 1920s Shanghai décor. With excellent service and a delectable menu of food and cocktails, it's perfect for families and those seeking a break from the city's bustling nightlife.

Address: The Lane (behind Pub Street)

Opening Hours: 6 p.m.

Asana Old Wooden House

This stylish venue provides a cultural and historical experience alongside your drink. Set in one of the few remaining Khmer wooden houses, it offers a relaxed atmosphere for sipping cocktails. The cocktails feature special local herbs and spices for a distinctive flavor, and you can even participate in a cocktail workshop to learn how to recreate their signature drinks.

Address: Street 7
Opening Hours: 12:00 p.m.

Naga Bar

If you appreciate high-quality cocktails and unique dining options, this is the place to be. Naga Bar offers exquisite cocktails and diverse dining choices at reasonable prices. With a more relaxed atmosphere, it's perfect for a comfortable pre-dinner cocktail and conversation with friends or family.

Address: Vithei Charles de Gaulle | Khum Svay Dang Kum, Le Méridien Angkor
Opening Hours: 4 p.m.

Siem Reap Prosecco Cocktails Bar

This outdoor bar with a laid-back island vibe is perfect for a tropical country like Cambodia. Nestled under the stars and surrounded by trees, it features simple wooden chairs and friendly service. The venue's simplicity adds to its charm and continues to attract satisfied customers who appreciate the warm atmosphere and friendly staff.

Address: Achar Sva St, Siem Reap 17259
Opening Hours: 6:30 p.m.

Le Siem Reap

Situated on the Siem Reap River waterfront, this unique bar offers high-quality and creative cocktails despite its small size. The bar exudes a friendly vibe and service, allowing you to enjoy the refreshing river breeze while sipping fresh cocktails in a relaxed setting.

Address: Opposite Angkor Trade Centre | Along Siem Reap Riverside, Old Market Area
Opening Hours: 7 p.m.

X Bar

A gem for young-spirited bar-goers on Pub Street, X Bar is a popular destination for both locals and foreigners. It hosts fantastic parties almost every night of the week and offers great live music and DJs. You can also enjoy an incredible view of the entire Pub Street from the rooftop.

Address: Rooftop at the end of Pub Street

Opening Hours: 4 p.m.

The Yellow Sub

True to its name, this four-floor Beatles-themed bar on The Lane is filled with Beatles and '60s memorabilia. You can expect good food, inexpensive drinks, and music from that era. The friendly staff bring the place to life every night.

Address: 9A, The Lane
Opening Hours: 11 a.m.

Foreign Correspondents Club Angkor

For a more upscale experience with a romantic ambiance, excellent service, and quality food and drinks, the FCC is an ideal choice. Situated within the renowned Foreign Correspondents Club Hotel, it features a beautifully-designed outdoor bar and restaurant, perfect for spending an evening with loved ones.

Address: Pokambor Avenue
Opening Hours: 11:00 a.m.

Picasso Bar

Picasso Bar is a well-known spot on Pub Street, known for its exceptional atmosphere. Live music, happy hours, and a friendly vibe make it an excellent place to linger. The outdoor seating area provides a perfect vantage point for watching the lively Pub Street scene.

Temple Club

Located near Pub Street, Temple Club occupies a colonial-style building that once served as the French Governor's residence. Its elegant charm and rich cultural history make it a favorite among both locals and tourists. Come for a delightful dining experience and stay for the lively DJ sets that typically start later in the night.

Mezze Lounge & Nightclub

This unconventional establishment offers a fusion of Lebanese, Mediterranean, and Italian influences and stays open until the early hours of the morning. Whether you want to savor delicious cocktails at a relaxed pace or lose yourself on the dance floor to the music, Mezze Lounge & Nightclub has you covered.

ACCOMMODATION OPTIONS

Best Neighborhoods to Stay

When you're deciding on accommodations in Siem Reap, it's essential to find a place with a pool, as the city can get scorching, especially when you're out exploring temples in the hot sun.

To help you choose the right neighborhood to stay in, here are five areas in Siem Reap that you might want to consider: the French Quarter, Old Market, Wat Bo, Taphul Village, or near Charles de Gaulle Boulevard. I've compiled a list of some of the best places to stay in Siem Reap for each of these areas.

1.Old French Quarter - Ideal for First-Time Visitors

The Old French Quarter is centrally located, offering a perfect blend of unique temples to explore during the day and lively nightclubs to enjoy in the evening. This neighborhood is the gateway to the stunning Angkor Wat, the largest religious monument globally, but it has much more to offer. With its mix of colonial buildings, traditional temples, and classic Chinese shop houses, the Old French Quarter exudes a multicultural atmosphere.

Due to its proximity to key attractions like the Royal Residence and the iconic Angkor Archaeological Park, many tourists prefer booking their hotels here. Be sure to make your reservations well in advance, as this area tends to be quite crowded.

Apart from its historical charm, the Old French Quarter is teeming with international cuisine restaurants and vibrant bars. So, once you've had a good rest, set out to explore this lively neighborhood.

Best Hotels in the Old French Quarter:

La Rivière d'Angkor Resort: Nestled amidst lush tropical gardens, this resort offers traditionally-decorated bungalows, a spacious outdoor pool, and an on-site restaurant serving delectable dishes. You can also pamper yourself with spa treatments or relax on the sun terrace when you're not exploring the Old French Quarter.

Chhay Long Angkor Boutique Hotel: For a clean, modern, and boutique experience, Chhay Long Angkor Boutique Hotel is an excellent choice. Located just three blocks away from Pub Street, it boasts a convenient location. You can also escape the heat of Southeast Asia in the great pool.

Park Hyatt: Situated in the heart of Siem Reap, within walking distance of the French Colonial Quarters, the Old Market, and Pub streets, the Park Hyatt offers luxurious 5-star accommodations. The hotel features an extensive collection of modern and traditional Cambodian art, indoor and outdoor pools, and three on-site dining options that prioritize local ingredients for environmentally-conscious guests.

Central Blanche Residence: This beautifully designed residence features a restaurant, an outdoor swimming pool, and a bar. Start your day with a buffet breakfast and end it with a fun game of billiards. Bikes are available for rent at the front desk, perfect for exploring Siem Reap and Angkor Wat.

The Night Hotel: With a lovely outdoor pool and landscaped garden, The Night Hotel offers a peaceful setting in the heart of Siem Reap. Tucked away for privacy, it's perfect for an Instagram-worthy experience. The on-site restaurant offers a slightly higher-priced but delicious menu, including dishes like amok or lemongrass soup.

Things to See and Do in the Old French Quarter:

Explore miniature replicas of Angkor's temples at the Miniature Replicas of Angkor's Temples.

Discover serenity at Preah Ang Chek Preah Ang Chom, a beautiful temple in the city center.

Savor contemporary Asian cuisine and a selection of wines at Cassia Restaurant.

Pass by the Royal Residence, the home of the Cambodian royals.

Cool down at Siem Reap Brewpub, a great spot for food, beer, and a fantastic atmosphere.

Dive into the history and culture of Siem Reap at the Angkor National Museum.

Enjoy authentic Cambodian cuisine at the chic and stylish Kroya Restaurant.

Take a short trip north of Siem Reap to experience the splendor of Angkor Wat.

2.Taphul Village - Best for Families

If you're traveling with kids and looking for accommodations close to central Siem Reap but away from the bustling city center, Taphul Village is an excellent choice. Located west of the Old French Quarter, it offers tranquility amidst the city's hustle and bustle.

In Taphul Village, you'll find yourself within walking distance of shopping malls and numerous restaurants. While the neighborhood doesn't have many attractions of its own, it boasts excellent public transport connections to Angkor Wat and other temples in the Old French Quarter, as well as the Royal Independence Gardens, where you can take your kids to play and enjoy some fresh air.

Best Hotels in Taphul Village:

Aroma Angkor: This boutique hotel features spacious family rooms with balconies leading to an outdoor swimming pool. Enjoy a family breakfast and explore various activities, such as cooking classes or bike tours with the kids.

Model Angkor Resort: Conveniently located in the heart of the city, this resort offers a swimming pool, poolside bar, restaurant, massage, and spa services. The tastefully decorated modern rooms ensure a comfortable stay.

Bou Savy Villa: With a 10-minute walk to Pub Street, Bou Savy Villa is well-placed for exploring the city's restaurants and bars. The small guesthouse offers personalized care with its 12 rooms, each equipped with air conditioning and a balcony. You'll love the lovely pool, perfect for a refreshing dip between temple visits.

Mulberry Boutique Hotel: This charming property is located in the heart of Siem Reap, providing modern and comfortable rooms, along with a swimming pool and a relaxing garden. It's the ideal place to unwind after a day of adventures.

Things to See and Do in Taphul Village:

Explore the Lucky Mall shops to escape the heat and find everything from toy stores to supermarkets.

Enjoy Asian fusion dishes at Lilypop, a centrally-located, family-friendly restaurant.

Satisfy your sweet tooth at Fresh Fruit Factory, a café offering handmade iced desserts, sweet treats, and tasty bites.

Watch the sunrise over Angkor Wat by heading north of the city.

Rent bikes for a day of exploring the towns, villages, and fields surrounding Siem Reap.

Visit Artbox, the world's largest and highest-level trick art museum, located just a short drive from the city.

Immerse yourself in Cambodian culture and heritage at the Cambodian Cultural Village.

3. Old Market – Ideal for Nightlife Enthusiasts

If you're looking to immerse yourself in Siem Reap's vibrant night markets and clubs, the Old Market is the place to be! Situated along the banks of the Siem Reap River, this neighborhood is renowned for its lively night markets and bustling nightlife. It's the go-to spot for shopping, dining, and entertainment after the sun goes down.

By day, you can explore the streets of this area, but the true magic of the Old Market unfolds after sunset amid the countless temple columns. Named after the actual Old Market, where you can shop for clothes, souvenirs, and a variety of goods, this area also boasts a beautiful Buddhist temple and gardens that are well worth a visit.

Located just a 15-minute drive away from the famous Angkor Temple, the Old Market area is directly connected to the road leading to the Angkor Wat Temple complex, making it a convenient choice for many visitors.

Best Hotels in Old Market:

Golden Temple Retreat: This remarkable residence is adorned with handcrafted elements and features an in-house restaurant. Guests can relax at the spa center, explore the garden, and take a dip in the outdoor swimming pool at this charming boutique hotel.

Entire Villa: Situated just 250 meters from the Old Market, this beautiful villa with a pool offers an oasis of tranquility in the midst of a bustling city. Run by a Cambodian family, it provides privacy, a relaxing pool, and easy access to everything you need.

Residence Wat Damnak: Located just across the river in Damnak, Residence Wat Damnak is a budget-friendly boutique hotel that's only a 3-minute walk from the Old Market. It offers great value, featuring two pools, a sauna, a hot tub, and two poolside restaurants. It's the ideal place for budget-conscious travelers who still want great amenities.

Golden Temple Retreat: If you're seeking accommodations away from the city's hustle and bustle, the Golden Temple Retreat is a fantastic choice. It boasts an outdoor swimming pool, an in-house restaurant, and bar. The spacious rooms with comfortable beds are complemented by the spa and swimming pool. The Golden Temple Retreat also offers complimentary two-way airport transfers.

Exploring the Old Market: Uncover Must-See Attractions and Exciting Activities

Explore Kendal Village, an up-and-coming area of Old Market with quaint cafes and trendy restaurants.

Dance the night away at BARCODE, a chic and stylish lounge featuring resident DJs spinning the hottest tunes.

Savor the evening with drinks at The Angkor Wat Bar, a laid-back and trendy spot nestled in the vibrant atmosphere of Pub Street.

Sip on contemporary cocktails at Miss Wong's Cocktail Bar, known for its chic décor and tasty drinks.

Shop for souvenirs, food, and drinks at the lively Angkor Night Market.

Unwind at the laid-back Laundry Bar after a day of sightseeing.

Relish Khmer cocktails at Asana, the city's only traditional Khmer house.

Head to Temple Club for a night of drinks and dancing until the early morning.

Experience exotic cocktails, great music, and a fun night out at YOLO Bar.

4. Charles de Gaulle Boulevard – Ideal for Luxury Seekers

For those seeking a luxurious experience in Siem Reap, Charles de Gaulle Boulevard is an excellent choice. This boulevard is lined with high-end hotels and resorts, making it one of the most exclusive places to stay in the city.

This area is perfect if you're past your partying days and prefer a quieter atmosphere with cultural attractions and shopping malls. The boulevard connects directly to the road leading to the Angkor Wat Temple complex, offering convenience to travelers looking to explore this iconic site.

Charles de Gaulle Boulevard features numerous gardens, providing a peaceful and scenic environment for those seeking a relaxing getaway. However, if you crave some evening entertainment, you can easily head to the Old French Quarter or Old Market.

Best Hotels in Charles De Gaulle Boulevard:

Templation Hotel: This luxury hotel in Siem Reap is a dream come true, surrounded by lush private gardens. The award-winning hotel offers an outdoor pool, an in-house restaurant, and a bar. Away from the city's hustle and bustle, this boutique property is an oasis of tranquility, where guests can unwind in the spa.

Saem Siem Reap Hotel: Just 15 minutes from the Angkor Temples and 5 minutes from Pub Street by tuk-tuk, the Saem Siem Reap Hotel is perfectly situated for luxury and relaxation. The hotel offers a breakfast buffet and an amazing pool. The polite and attentive staff add to the elegance of this hotel, all at very affordable prices.

Raffles Grand Hotel D'angkor: The Raffles Grand Hotel d'Angkor offers elegant accommodations in the heart of Siem Reap. It features a lap pool, a fitness center, a spa, and four on-site dining options. Activities such as yoga and Khmer dance are also available. If you're seeking opulent lodging and top-tier services, you've just stumbled upon your ideal destination.

5. Wat Bo – Perfect for Budget Travelers

If you're in search of affordable places to stay in Siem Reap, look no further than Wat Bo, an area that caters to budget-conscious travelers. This neighborhood, located across the Siem Reap River from the Old French Quarter, is home to one of the city's oldest temples, which gives the area its name. Wat Bo also features unique art galleries showcasing local artists' work and offering workshops.

Additionally, Wat Bo enjoys a convenient location within walking distance of the city center, where you'll find more art galleries and other attractions. The area is known for its green spaces, colorful flower decorations, and a relaxed atmosphere, making it an inviting place to spend your time.

Best Hotels in Wat Bo:

Viroth's Hotel: This hotel boasts contemporary and minimalist design and is surrounded by lush greenery. When you're not out exploring Wat Bo, you can relax by the swimming pool or enjoy delicious food at the on-site restaurant after a spa session. The rooms are beautifully decorated with Cambodian artifacts and provide ample space.

Riversoul Residence: Riversoul Residence is a four-star hotel located in the heart of the Wat Bo Road area. It's a short walk to the heart of Siem Reap, near Pub Street, the Night Market, and trendy nightspots. The modern and comfortable rooms are outfitted with all the necessities for a relaxing stay.

Two Dragons: If you're on a budget, you'll love Two Dragons, a budget-friendly spot near Angkor Wat and Pub Street. The guesthouse offers a fun way to explore Angkor and the surrounding area with bicycle rentals.

Oriental Siem Reap: This beautiful guesthouse is tucked away on a quiet street in the Wat Bo area. It's about a 15-minute walk to Pub Street or a 2-minute tuk-tuk ride away. The resort features a swimming pool, a restaurant/bar, a gym, and a full-service spa. This is a great place to spend the morning temple hopping and the hot afternoon by the pool.

Eocambo Residence: Located away from the hustle and bustle of Pub Street, eOcambo Residence in the Wat Bo area provides a comfortable stay with features like currency exchange, WiFi, free breakfast, a beautiful pool, and a sauna. This is the ultimate haven for thrifty adventurers, making it a superb pick for those mindful of their travel budget.

Exploring Wat Bo: Unveiling the Best Sights and Activities

Enjoy delectable meals at Hansa BBQ & Seafood.

Marvel at the beauty of Wat Bo Temple, one of the oldest and most exquisite temples in the province.

Savor affordable traditional Khmer dishes at Khmer Grill Restaurant.

Explore the colorful and relaxing riverside by renting bikes.

Experience a spectacular stage show at the Angkor Village Apsara Theatre, featuring music, dance, and singing.
Visit the Siem Reap Art Centre Market, where you can find everything from pedicures to exotic foods.

Pamper yourself with a relaxing spa day at Seasons Spa.

Enjoy the beauty of the Wat Damnak Buddhist Temple's stunning architecture and décor.

Sip on Sombai, a sweet Cambodian liqueur for an authentic taste of Siem Reap.

Take a three-hour boat tour down the Siem River to see the city and countryside from a new angle.

6. Wat Damnak – The Coolest Place to Stay in Siem Reap

Wat Damnak, a small neighborhood on the east side of the river, south of Wat Bo Road, is a tranquil and relaxing area. It's conveniently located near the Angkor Night Market and the lively bars of Pub Street. Well-connected to the rest of the city, Wat Damnak is an up-and-coming district with renowned restaurants and cafes serving contemporary and modern cuisines.

This neighborhood is perfect for enjoying great food, a few drinks, and relaxation in the heart of the city.

Best Hotel in Wat Damnak:

Bophus Residence: Bophus Residence is a stunning four-star hotel in Wat Damnak, featuring 20 spacious and modern rooms. Guests can access a relaxing outdoor pool and seating area. The hotel is centrally located, surrounded by restaurants and bars, and a short walk to the city's top attractions.

Things to See and Do in Wat Damnak:

Savor exquisite dishes at Cuisine Wat Damnak, one of the city's most famous restaurants.

Indulge in Euro-Asian fusion cuisine at The Republic, a rustic and relaxing restaurant.

Explore the Siem Reap Art Centre Market to browse stalls offering everything from pedicures to exotic foods.

Treat yourself to a spa day at Seasons Spa.

Enjoy a unique performance at Bambu Stage Siem Reap in a tropical garden theater.

Sample Sombai, a sweet Cambodian liqueur, for an authentic Siem Reap experience.

Admire the beautiful architecture and décor of the Wat Damnak Buddhist Temple.

Satisfy your taste buds with delicious and budget-friendly traditional Khmer dishes at Khmer Grill Restaurant.

BEST TRAVEL RESOURCES

The top travel resources I often utilize are as follows:

My all-time favorite tool for finding flights is **SkyScanner.** It always seems to find the best deals, and its calendar display lets you know which days are the least expensive for travel. Since it searches obscure booking websites that no one else does, it appeals to me. Start here for all of your flight searches.

Momodo: This wonderful website does extensive airline searches, including a number of low-cost flights that larger websites go over. Even though Skyscanner is where I generally start, I'll check this website to compare prices.

Google Flights: To find the cheapest destination, enter your departure airport and explore flights all across the world on a map using Google Flights. This search engine is helpful for finding routes, connections, and costs.

Hostelworld is the most user-friendly hostel booking website on the market, offering the largest selection, the best search functionality, and the most availability. Additionally, you may search for private or shared beds. For my reservations, I utilize it.

Using the website **Couchsurfing**, you may stay in peoples' spare rooms or on their couches for no cost. It's a great opportunity to meet people who can educate you a lot more about a region than a hostel or hotel can while also saving money. Additionally, there are online communities where you may plan to meet up for local events.

Booking.com is a great place to find inexpensive hotels and various types of housing. I appreciate the simplicity of the user interface.

Trusted Housesitters: For a fun (and cost-free) way to vacation, consider house- or pet-sitting. In exchange for free housing, you just look after someone else's house and/or pet while they are away. It's a great option for budget-conscious people and long-term visitors.

CONCLUSION

As we conclude this travel guide to Siem Reap, we reflect on the remarkable journey through this captivating city and its surrounding wonders. Siem Reap, a destination with a rich history, culture, and natural beauty, offers travelers an unforgettable experience. From the awe-inspiring temples of Angkor to the vibrant markets, serene neighborhoods, and luxurious getaways, Siem Reap has something to offer every type of traveler.

Unveiling Angkor's Mysteries

Our journey began with the crown jewel of Siem Reap, the Angkor Archaeological Park. Angkor Wat, the world's largest religious monument, stands as a testament to the ingenuity and devotion of the Khmer people.

As the sun casts its warm glow over the temple, travelers from across the globe gather to witness a sight that transcends time and space. But the Angkor complex is not limited to just Angkor Wat; the smiling faces of Bayon, the delicate beauty of Ta Prohm, and the hidden treasures of Banteay Srei beckon explorers to delve deeper into the heart of Khmer history.

The temples, adorned with intricate carvings and surrounded by lush jungles, offer a connection to the past that is both humbling and inspiring.

Where to Stay: From Budget to Luxury

Our guide also provided insights into the various neighborhoods of Siem Reap, each with its unique character and charm.

The Old French Quarter, with its colonial architecture and bustling streets, offers a blend of history and modernity. It's the ideal place for those looking to be at the heart of the city's action.

Taphul Village, on the other hand, is a peaceful haven for families, offering easy access to shopping and cultural attractions.

For those seeking a touch of luxury and tranquility, Charles de Gaulle Boulevard is the perfect choice. This boulevard, lined with high-end hotels and beautiful gardens, offers a serene retreat for those looking to explore the temples at their own pace.

Wat Bo, a budget traveler's paradise, combines affordability with a convenient location. It's a place where you can experience local culture and still enjoy modern comforts.

Beyond Temples: Exploring the Local Culture

Siem Reap is not just about temples; it's a city teeming with life and local culture. We've taken you to vibrant markets, charming cafes, and contemporary art galleries where you can engage with the community and witness the creative spirit of Siem Reap.

The local cuisine, a harmonious blend of flavors and spices, invites you to embark on a culinary adventure. From street food stalls to stylish restaurants, the Khmer dishes are a delight for the senses.

Activities for Every Adventurer

Whether you're an explorer, a food enthusiast, a history buff, or simply someone seeking relaxation, Siem Reap caters to your interests. Beyond temple-hopping, you can explore the floating villages of Tonle Sap Lake, take a balloon ride for a breathtaking aerial view, or indulge in activities such as cycling, hiking, and even bird-watching in the surrounding natural reserves.

The Heartwarming Cambodian Spirit

Perhaps the most remarkable aspect of Siem Reap is its people. The warmth and resilience of the Cambodian spirit are evident in the smiles of the locals. Despite a history marked by adversity, the people of Siem Reap have embraced tourism as a means of rebuilding their lives.

Their genuine hospitality and enthusiasm are a testament to their unwavering spirit.

A Sustainable Journey

As you journey through Siem Reap, we encourage you to travel responsibly. Be mindful of the fragile environments and the communities that depend on the tourism industry.

Embrace eco-friendly practices, support local artisans, and engage with the culture in a respectful manner. By doing so, you can ensure that Siem Reap remains a welcoming and sustainable destination for future generations of travelers.

In conclusion, Siem Reap is a place where ancient traditions and modern aspirations coexist harmoniously. The city's soul lies not just in its awe-inspiring temples but also in its vibrant markets, serene neighborhoods, and the welcoming smiles of its people.

We hope this travel guide has enriched your Siem Reap journey and inspired you to embark on an adventure that will leave you with lifelong memories. Whether you're exploring the temples, savoring Khmer cuisine, or simply taking in the local culture, Siem Reap is a destination that will touch your heart and soul.

So pack your bags, embrace the magic of Siem Reap, and create your own unforgettable story in this enchanting corner of the world.

Printed in Great Britain
by Amazon

43910362R00079